A Practical Guide to Death & Dying

John White

A PRACTICAL GUIDE
to Death & Dying

*This publication made possible with
the assistance of the Kern Foundation*

The Theosophical Publishing House
Wheaton, Ill. U.S.A.
Madras, India/London, England

The Theosophical Publishing House
306 West Geneva Road
Wheaton, IL 60187

A publication of the Theosophical Publishing House, a department of the Theosophical Society in America.

Library of Congress Cataloging-in-Publication Data

White, John Warren, 1939-
    A practical guide to death & dying.

    Bibliography: p.
    1. Death. 2. Theosophy. I. Title. II. Title:
Practical guide to death and dying.
BP573.D4W48   1988   291.2'3   88-40134
ISBN 0-8356-0633-3

Printed in the United States of America

With affection and gratitude for their lessons in living,
this book is dedicated to my parents,
Jane and Robert White
and to my parents-in-law,
Dorothy Devin and her late husband, Bill.

. . . so few know the art of dying. For dying, like living, is an art and if only most of us mastered the art of dying as much as we seek to master the art of living, there would be many more happy deaths.

The fact of the matter, however, is that the art of living is not different from the art of dying; in fact, the one flows into the other, and cannot be separated one from the other. He who has mastered the art of living has already mastered the art of dying; to such, death holds no terrors.

M.V. Kamath,
*Philosophy of
Death and Dying*

*When you were born you cried
And the whole world rejoiced.
Live such a life that when you die
The whole world cries and you rejoice.*
Traditional Indian saying

Contents

Preface

Death—the great unknown, the final frontier. People regard it with fascination, loathing, fear. From Halloween skeletons and ghosts through soap opera heroines in peril to political assassinations and war stories, death is a perennial topic of conversation, drama, and news. Lately, it has also become the subject of feature stories, college courses, public conferences, and best-selling books.

Death is everywhere and, like the weather, it seems not much can be done about it. At least, that was the attitude until recently. Years ago, W.C. Fields could joke, "This world's a hard place. A fella's lucky to get out of it alive." In the past decade, however, for a variety of reasons many people have seriously entertained thoughts of "doing something" about death.

First, there were biomedical advances. Heart and other organ transplants—real and artificial—gave prolonged life to ailing people. New medicines and vaccines tamed many traditionally-dreaded illnesses. Sophisticated technology kept people alive, albeit in a vegetative-like coma, even when vital signs had disappeared altogether.

At the same time, a movement arose called "death education." Its purpose: to dignify death and humanize its fearfulness. Its premise: understanding death can enhance the quality of life and expand our consciousness of existence. In the medical and helping professions, thanatology grew out of psychological concern for the dying and the bereaved. Paralleling this, the consumer

movement took the funeral industry to task for preying
upon grief-dulled and unsuspecting families by manipu-
lating them into buying overpriced, unnecessary products
and services. Euthanasia or mercy killing made front page
news during some sensational murder trials, as did the
ensuing debate over legislation that would allow people
the right to die under certain circumstances. Likewise,
opponents of capital punishment made headlines, forcing
public debate about death. Parapsychology, which had
begun humbly in the last century as psychic researchers
studied the question of life after death, came boldly to
public notice with startling new evidence of postmortem
survival. And the immortalist movement, proclaiming death
"a grave mistake," declared that people would some day
live forever.

All this has served a useful and healthy purpose. It has
"opened up" the subject of death and dying and made it
respectable to discuss. No longer need you be considered
morbid or in bad taste for talking about it in public. Even
Dear Abby puts it in her column! Nevertheless, the clinical
reports, poignant anecdotes and exhaustive statistical
studies somehow fail to address the most basic fear we all
have: the fear of *we ourselves* dying. All the research, all
the death education seems to be telling us about *someone
else* dying. We've been told in theoretical terms about the
emotional stages a dying person goes through. We've been
told in personal terms how to share the grief of others
when they lose a loved one. We've been told how parents
can explain death to children, and how the clergy and
physicians can counsel the dying. But no one has really
described systematically how we ourselves can begin to
deal honestly and intelligently with the fear of our *own*
nonbeing, annihilation, self-extinction.

That is what I will do here. This book is intended for
people who feel as the poet Keats did in his sonnet, "When
I have fears that I may cease to be. . . ." It will provide
practical instructions and experiential situations—real
"how to" learning conditions—in which to explore the
biology, psychology and metaphysics of your own death.

It will also provide intellectually-satisfying information about life after death. In addition, you'll find the inspiring wisdom of many courageous people who have eliminated the fear of dying from their lives and have then stood forth as models of the highest potential in people to live selflessly and nobly for human betterment.

In short, this book takes a multileveled, comprehensive approach to providing real self-help through a program of personal action. You can work with it on your own, in the quiet of your room, without a guide or facilitator, and without the need for group experiences until you're ready for them. Information, inspiration, insight and personal experience are the keys offered here for unlocking the hope, health and happiness so long imprisoned in so many people by their mortal terror of oblivion. You are going to turn your fear of death into the death of fear, and begin to really *live*!

1
The Difference between Death and Dying

Most people are so afraid of dying that they're scared to live. And that is the difference between death and dying. Death is a *biological* process, a function of the body. Dying is a *psychological* process, a function of the mind.

As a biological process, death is part of the wisdom of the body. It is given by nature to every living thing, and occurs without their having to learn anything or do anything. It is inherent in embodied existence, or at least—to acknowledge the immortalists—it has been until now. As Ecclesiastes said, "To every thing there is a season . . . a time to be born and a time to die. . . ." The laws of physiology which produced the organism are the same laws which terminate it, and even though the termination may appear inexplicable or absurd, death is an undeniable "fact of life."

Only humans are afraid to die. All other organisms expire without fear. That's not to say they don't struggle to live if they find themselves in life-threatening circumstances. The rabbit flees the fox, the fish fights the hook, the bayed panther slashes at the hunter, the bird tries to escape the snare. But these actions are instinctive and unpremeditated. Among animals, there is no gnawing anxiety in advance of death.

There is a special reason for this. You see, animals don't have a sense of time with which to anticipate their future demise. They live strictly in the present, the here-and-now. Nor do animals have a sense of self—an ego—which can be mentally projected into future circumstances. It is, therefore, psychologically impossible for animals to fear the loss of their life as humans do. Just as it instinctively fights to live in life-threatening circumstances, when an animal reaches the end of old age, it instinctively goes off by itself to die or allows itself to be killed, without fighting the circumstances and without fear. It accepts what is to happen as naturally as it previously fought to live. There is no argument about it, no denial of it, no refusal, no bargaining, no self-pity. When it happens, it happens—unforeseen but, from the animal's point of view, entirely proper.

Animals live in the simple present; humans do not. Animals have no self-image or self-identity; humans do. And that is the crux of the problem. That is the difference between death and dying. That is the source of human suffering and misery. "Will you realize once for all," said the Greek philosopher Epictetus, "that it is not death that is the source of all man's evils, and of a mean and cowardly spirit, but rather the fear of death? Against this fear then I would have you discipline yourself; to this let all your reasonings, your lectures, and your trainings be directed; and then you will know that only so do men achieve their freedom."

How many people do you know who truly live freely, robustly and joyfully, without fear of death? Probably not many—if any. Judging by what I see, most people have some degree of chronic anxiety about their eventual demise, and it's oftentimes a crippling, paralyzing degree. Isn't that why the life insurance industry is doing so well? Basically, when you buy it you're betting that you won't live to a ripe old age. But that's a foolish attitude because, statistically speaking, if the odds weren't *for* you rather than against you, life insurance companies would be out of business. They'd be paying out more money than they take in, and would very quickly go bankrupt.

Of course, you never can tell when your number is up, as they say. Death may come by illness, accident, murder, war, or natural disaster long before you reach old age. With rare exceptions, you never know how, you never know when. And so some people buy life insurance even if they aren't especially "uptight" about dying because the thought of unexpectedly leaving a spouse and family without income or savings is reason enough. I know—I'm in this category.

In far greater numbers, though, are those whose days and nights are spent fearfully building psychological—rather than economic—defenses against the reality of death and what they think will be their eventual non-existence—the total disappearance of their being and identity. Their years go by in joyless flight from all adventure, all risk, all opportunity for growth and free self-expression. Their principal concern seems always to be safety and security. Anything that might involve danger or pain is avoided politely and even, if necessary, vehemently. Anything that might require them to "open up" their constricted and closely guarded little island-self is withdrawn from or shunned. Thus, defense by defense, they deny death. They push it out of their minds, thinking for a while that it will "save" them from the Grim Reaper.

"But at my back I always hear/Time's winged chariot hurrying near," the poet Andrew Marvell wrote three centuries ago, and it is still true. We still "hear" time passing—even as we deny it. Thus, the continued denial of death requires ever-stronger defenses. And so, many people retreat into alcohol, drugs, promiscuity, depression, insanity. These are all ways in which we try to deny time and mortality by "getting high" or "out of our minds" or "retreating to the womb."

Denial of death also takes forms that have been institutionalized in our culture as acceptable, even desirable. Much of what we regard as great human achievement has been shown through depth psychology to be unconsciously prompted by a flight from death. Art, economics, politics, architecture—would you believe that fear of death is behind them? That is exactly what so much of modern psychology has demonstrated. Our strivings for permanence and stability are really strivings for immortality. Heaven-reaching skyscrapers are monuments in stone and steel memorializing the architect; paintings and sculpture do the same for their creators. Fame, wealth, status, titles, possessions, power—these, too, are ways in which we try unconsciously to deny death and to assert that we shall not perish from the earth. But no matter how we disguise it, said Ernest Becker in *The Denial of Death*, the fear of death is "the basic fear that influences all others, a fear from which no one is immune. . . ." It haunts the human animal like nothing else, he says, adding that it is "a main-spring of human activity—activity designed largely to avoid the fatality of death, to overcome it by denying in some way that it is the final destiny of man."

Freud was one of the first in contemporary psychology to look at death with an unswerving eye and see humanity's flight from death. He saw the desperate search to "make a name for yourself" as ways people unconsciously deny their eventual demise and attempt to live forever. "Our own death," he wrote, "is indeed unimaginable, and when-ever we make the attempt to imagine it we can perceive that we really survive as spectators. Hence . . . at bottom no one believes in his own death, or to put the same thing another way, in the unconscious every one of us is con-vinced of his own immortality."

Now, this is a curious remark—and a very hopeful one, although Freud did not intend it so. He was, as is well known, a pessimist who lived stoically but with little hope for humanity's improvement and eventual well-being. Religion is an illusion and death is the end, he said. But Freud will not have the last word in this book. For we have learned a great deal since, and it reveals an ironic twist in the whole game—a twist that offers an opportunity to turn our old enemy, death, into a friend. Into, in fact, our very *best* friend!

To understand what I mean by that, you'll have to read on. For in later chapters we are indeed going to imagine our own death. We are going to "die" and find that death is good. I'm sure Freud would have been delighted. Near the end of his life, he became a member of the British Society for Psychical Research and wrote to a colleague, "If I had my life to live over again, I should devote myself to psychical research rather than psychoanalysis." The next chapter will show you why.

2

The Scientific Evidence for Life After Death

Most people believe in life after death. The concept of post-mortem survival has been with us at least since the Neanderthal people 100,000 years ago began burying their dead and anointing them with reddish earth. Since that time, all the world's major religious, spiritual, and mystical traditions have maintained the reality of life after death.

But do they really *know*? Is their belief valid or merely fantasy or wishful thinking?

Faith and knowledge are not incompatible. Buddha advised his followers, "Believe nothing which is unreasonable, but reject nothing as unreasonable without proper examination." Likewise St. Peter, in his second epistle (1:4), admonished believers to support their faith with knowledge.

The purpose of this chapter is to give a *rational* basis to faith. That is because faith can be rational or irrational. Although most Americans believe in an afterlife—recent Gallup and Roper polls found that 70% did—their belief has little strength behind it. It is largely based on indoctrination they received, consciously or otherwise, as they grew up. That's not to say there's no truth to what they believe—only that they believe something without understanding its basis. They haven't "done their homework" by investigating the subject, examining the evidence and testing the validity of their belief. They have faith without knowledge—irrational or blind faith—and therefore only the weakest conviction that they will survive death.

Rational belief grows out of one's experience and reason. It's supported by factual information and it's tested—insofar as possible—by the scientific method. When it comes to the facts about whether we survive death, most people are quite uninformed.

In this chapter I'll demonstrate that there is almost a mountain of evidence, obtained competently and without bias during a full century of psychic research by hundreds of independent investigators in many countries. Altogether, this survival evidence provides the basis for a rational, scientifically-based belief in life after death.

Now, I'm not saying that the reality of an afterlife is proven as conclusively as you can prove a geometry problem. But the evidence strongly supports it—much more strongly than any other hypotheses for explaining the data. The evidence suggests that death can be compared to the change of state H_2O undergoes when water turns to steam. In other words, it's there, but you don't see it. (What you see coming out of a boiling teakettle isn't steam, incidentally. It's water vapor—condensed steam.)

Moreover, from the point of view of death as an altered state of consciousness, it seems that the quality of our continued existence in the afterlife depends very much on the quality of our living here and now—the degree to which we have grown in spiritual awareness and refinement of character. In other words, *the real importance of the evidence for life after death is that it can affect the quality and style of your life here and now.* And that is the purpose of this book—to help people who are so afraid of dying that they're scared to live.

With this in mind, let's look at the evidence for life after death. This evidence is what lends credence to the ancient idea of soul. Because of space requirements, I've summarized it in a highly compressed fashion. The evidence falls into eight major categories. Each category is derived independently of the others, so you can't discredit one and say that all the rest are false. Each category stands on its own. The eight categories are:

1. Mediumship
2. Apparitions of the dead
3. Out-of-body experiences
4. Reincarnation memories
5. Spirit photographs and spirit voice recordings
6. Possession cases
7. Deathbed observations
8. Near-death experiences

Mediumship

Mediums are people who claim to be able to contact the spirits of the dead, usually through direct mental communication, but also through automatic writing. (Ouija boards are sometimes used by people just beginning to dabble in mediumship, but I strongly warn you against this because you can get into serious difficulties from not knowing what you are doing.) Mediumship has been investigated since the beginning of psychic research in the late 1800s, and there have been many cases of paranormal information coming through, apparently from the deceased themselves. One famous case involved the English medium, Mrs. Gladys Leonard, and a ten-year-old boy, Bobby Newlove, who had died of diphtheria.

Mrs. Leonard had never met any member of the family and knew almost nothing about them. Yet her sittings (seances) gave highly appropriate and characteristic statements from Bobby, and they contained specific facts not conceivably within her normal knowledge. Some of the information wasn't even known to the family itself. Mrs. Leonard mentioned some pipes near a place where Bobby often played, saying that his health had been undermined by his playing with some contaminated water flowing from the pipes. A check by a medical officer determined that the water was contaminated and that an acute infection might result from drinking it. Following up still more clues given in the sittings, it was learned from Bobby's friend, Jack, that he and Bobby had played with the water.

Another mediumistic piece of evidence for life after death is called the cross-correspondences. These communications began about 1906 and continued for thirty-two years in three countries. They were apparently initiated by F.W.H. Myers, a noted psychic researcher who died in 1901. In the cross-correspondences, a dozen mediums produced disjointed and seemingly meaningless statements that nevertheless turned out to refer to common themes such as a Greek play or a poem known to Myers, who was also a professor of classics at Cambridge University. The obvious relations between many of the items produced by the mediums make the communications more than just chance occurrences. There were striking correspondences across countries and across decades, among mediums who didn't even know each other. The information they brought through was often beyond the educational background of the mediums, but it was familiar to Myers. Moreover, it was flavored by his attitude and personal style. Only when all the pieces were put together did it make sense to assume that a discarnate entity was communicating intelligently in a coordinated way that was supposed to demonstrate survival.

Apparitions of the Dead

Apparitions of the dead is the official term for ghosts, as distinguished from apparitions of the living (which we'll look at under "out-of-body experiences"). Not all ghosts are the haunting type. Only when an apparition is seen continually at a single location is it termed a haunting. Poltergeists are a certain type of haunting in which violent events and physical displays by an unseen force take place.

Crisis apparitions are different from hauntings. In a crisis, someone who has just died is seen by others in circumstances where the people usually aren't aware of the person's death until the apparition appears. Jesus appearing on the road to Emmaeus is an example. Another Biblical example of apparitions—but not a crisis apparition—is found in the gospels, where Jesus invited three disciples to go with him to a mountain top. There, as the Bible describes it, Moses and Elijah "appeared in glory" and spoke to Jesus.

Another case is the one that has been labeled "the scratched cheek case" because of the peculiar evidence offered. It seems a man whose initials were F.G. had a sister who died. Nine years later, he saw her apparition, and it was disfigured by a long red scratch on its cheek. F.G. reported this to his parents, and his mother nearly collapsed. It turned out that when the mother paid her last respects, she had tried to "touch up" her daughter's face and accidentally scratched the girl's cheek. She hid the accident with makeup, and only she knew of the incident.

Apparitions are real, although apparently nonphysical. They are seen fully clothed; they often appear in conjunction with material objects (such as holding something); they walk through walls; they may be seen collectively; they have been known to move physical objects; and they have been seen reflected in mirrors. Thus they appear to occupy real space while nevertheless being nonmaterial.

One of the most dramatic recent cases involves Dr. Elisabeth Kübler-Ross, the famous author of *On Death and Dying*. One of her deceased patients, Mary Schwartz, appeared in a fully materialized form in the corridor of a Chicago hospital in 1969. This was ten and a half months after she had died. She said to Kübler-Ross, who has told this story to lecture audiences, "Dr. Ross, I want to take two minutes of your time. Can we walk to your office?" Kübler-Ross began to conduct "reality testing" on herself as they went to the office to assure herself that she wasn't hallucinating.

As they reached the office, Mary opened the door and entered. Kübler-Ross sat at her desk. Mary closed the door, walked over and stood in front of the desk. She said, "I came back to thank you and Rennie Gaines (a minister who was in attendance when Mary was dying) for helping me to die, but my major reason is to tell you not to stop this work now. The time is not right." Kübler-Ross had been feeling frustrated and considered stopping her work with the dying because of the opposition she had encountered among her colleagues. And now an apparition was telling her what was going on in her own mind. At that point, as Kübler-Ross described it to one audience, "I did something shrewd in my desperation to obtain proof that this was real." She lied to Mary Schwartz, saying she needed a note to send to Rennie Gaines. Actually, she planned to keep the note herself to compare signatures.

So she handed Mary a pencil and piece of paper, and asked if she would write a note for him. Mary appeared to be full of love, Kübler-Ross said, and smiled as though she knew why her former doctor really wanted the note. She said, "Of course," wrote the message, signed her name, moved back from the desk, looked at Kübler-Ross, and asked, "You promise you'll not give up this work?" Kübler-Ross promised. Then Mary walked to the door, opened it, walked out and closed the door behind her. Kübler-Ross ran immediately to the door, opened it, but saw only an empty corridor. Nevertheless, this incident convinced Kübler-Ross of the reality of life after death. It marked a turning point in her work, and is the impulse behind what she is doing today. She now states, "The real job is . . . to tell people that death does not exist. It is very important that mankind knows that, because we are at the beginning of a very difficult time—not only for this country, but for the whole planet Earth."

Out-of-Body Experiences

The older terms for this phenomenon are astral projection and astral travel. They all refer to an experience of seeming to be in a place separate from one's physical body while fully and normally conscious. The experience can be either spontaneous or induced, and is frequently associated with crisis situations in its spontaneous form. OBEs are a universal human phenomenon, having been experienced in every time and culture. The effect on a person who has an OBE is almost always a conviction of survival after death. One such case involved a British soldier, Capt. Burton, who "died" one evening. That is, he lost all clinical signs of life—no pulse, no breath, etc. His doctor thought him lost, but he survived his heart failure and lived for many years after. He had a strange story to tell. He said, "I found myself standing at the foot of my bed, looking at myself and the doctor and feeling very well and bright, though puzzled. Then suddenly I found myself dragged violently over the bedrail where I floated above myself; following which came a tremendous crash. Then I heard the doctor's voice saying, 'He is coming round.' He had considered me dead for some time."

This story, which comes from the annals of psychic research, is like the dozens of cases collected by Dr. Raymond Moody in his books, *Life After Life* and *Reflections on Life After Life*. He was motivated to begin his research by Dr. George Ritchie, a Virginia psychiatrist, who himself had such an experience, many times more dramatic than Burton's, and who told it in 1978 in his book, *Return from Tomorrow*. The vehicle for this mobile, perceiving center of consciousness is sometimes called the astral body, the etheric body, the energy body, or the subtle body. It is reportedly connected to the flesh body by a thin silvery cord, though not everyone who "flies" sees such a thing.

Recently the American Society for Psychical Research in New York City has been studying OBEs, and has been quite successful in getting reports from people who claim to have the ability to project their consciousness this way. One of the star "fliers," Dr. Alex Tanous of Portland, Maine, was able with a high degree of accuracy to project to a remote point in space and tell what he saw through the viewing window of a special device built by the ASPR. It was constructed in such a way as to rule out the possibility of general clairvoyance. The scene viewed through the window was composed of images from two randomly-controlled picture wheels inside the device that projected their images through special lenses to a point in space about ten inches in front of the device. Even if you were in the same room, you couldn't see the composite picture except at that precise location, nor could you tell what the picture was just by using clairvoyance to look inside the device.

Tanous recently demonstrated out-of-body projection at the ASPR by viewing images inside a sealed 18-inch steel chamber. While Tanous was viewing a series of pictures, sensitive measuring devices inside the chamber recorded unusual energy effects.

OBEs seem to be a major key to understanding a psychic phenomenon called "apparitions of the living," in which a nonphysical image of someone still alive is seen in a location remote from where he is at that moment. This is formally termed bilocation—the full materialization of the out-of-body consciousness. The case of a recently-deceased Italian priest, Padre Pio, is a good example. One day this celebrated holy man, who had many other psychic events attributed to him, was celebrating mass when he remembered that he had promised to deliver a sermon elsewhere. He excused himself to the congregation, knelt at the altar, and pulled his hood over his head. At the same time, while he was in full view there, the congregation at the second church saw him appear, deliver the sermon, and then disappear.

Reincarnation Memories

Reincarnation is not the same as the transmigration of souls—the idea that a human can come back to earth life as an animal or some lower organism. Reincarnation means that a human soul comes back to earth in a human body, either because it hasn't fully learned the lessons it is supposed to or because, in the case of a highly spiritual person, it has a special task to perform in helping others.

One of the foremost authorities on reincarnation memories is Dr. Ian Stevenson, a psychiatrist who heads the division of parapsychology at the University of Virginia School of Medicine. Here is one of the most suggestive cases in Stevenson's files, as he tells it in his book, *Twenty Cases Suggestive of Reincarnation*. A five-year-old boy named Imad Elawar lived in a Middle East village. When he was less than two, Imad made references to a past life. He insisted he had lived in another village twenty-five miles away, and was a member of the Bouhamzy family there. In 1964 Stevenson took Imad and his father to the second village. Townspeople there recalled an Ibrahim Bouhamzy, who had died of tuberculosis nine years before Imad's birth. Imad also gave descriptions of his house and life before they went to the village. When they got there, Stevenson found that these descriptions were exact. One of Imad's first words as an infant had been "Jamileh." Imad's parents had no idea what that meant, but Stevenson learned that Ibrahim, who had never married, had kept a beautiful mistress named Jamileh.

In assessing this case, Stevenson said that the possibility of fraud is so small that it can be dismissed. The only other possible explanation, he said, is reincarnation. In a recent interview, he summed up his years of investigation by saying, "I don't think we have proof of reincarnation—nothing like certainties. But there is an impressive body of evidence." And, he adds, nothing else explains it better.

Another case—this one recorded by the widely-regarded Indian holy man, Swami Sivananda, in his book, *What Becomes of the Soul after Death?*—centered on Shanti Devi, an Indian girl born in 1926. While very young she recalled vivid memories of her previous life from 1902-25. These memories included details of events and experiences with her husband in that life, a pundit named Kedar Nath Chaubey. The little girl eventually insisted that her parents take her to the city of her previous birth. There the girl instantly recognized Kedar Chaubey as her previous husband. She also recognized her ten-year-old son, her old friends, and the building and the temple where she had worshipped. She also recalled that she had hidden about one hundred rupees, intending to give them to the temple. But she had died before she could make the donation. When she went to the hiding place and dug for the money, she was dismayed not to find it. Then Kedar Chaubey confessed that he had taken the money after the death of his former wife.

An equally strange form of reincarnation memory goes under the name xenoglossy. This is the spontaneous production of foreign languages unknown to the speaker. But it is not the ordinary speaking in tongues. In a few rare cases, the speaker produces a language no longer used on Earth.

The Rosemary Case was generated by a trance medium, Rosemary, of Blackpool, England, during the period from 1928 to 1961. She began to speak the language of the people of Egypt during the Eighteenth Dynasty, some 1400 years before Christ. She produced a large volume of the language, which was recorded and transcribed by competent linguists, who examined it and found that Rosemary was giving them new knowledge about the language— knowledge about Egyptian pronunciation and grammar that had been lost for centuries. She was helping the linguists on tough points they had been debating for years. Interestingly, Rosemary claimed that she had also picked up a personal memory of one of her prior lives—as a priestess in the famous Temple of Karnak—when she began to speak in this long-forgotten Egyptian tongue.

In his book, *My Land and My People*, the Dalai Lama of Tibet describes the procedure that took place when he was selected to his office. This case illustrates the "special task" I mentioned in the case of highly spiritual people.

Following indications expressed by the 13th Dalai Lama before he died which told the district in which he expected to be reborn, a committee was set up to make a search. The committee went to the district and there they found a three-year-old boy, who appeared to fulfill the conditions. The committee brought with them two identical black rosaries, one of which had belonged to the 13th Dalai Lama.

When they offered these to the boy, he chose the one which was his in the previous incarnation, and put it around his neck. A similar test was completed successfully with yellow rosaries. Then they offered him two drums, a very small one used for calling attendants, and an ornate, attractive drum with golden straps. He chose the former and began to beat it in the way which is customary during prayers. Finally, they presented two walking sticks to the boy. He touched the first one and looked at it with hesitation. Then he took the other and held it firmly in his hand. The hesitation had arisen through an interesting fact—the former Dalai Lama had originally used the first walking stick, but had subsequently given it to another lama.

Spirit Photographs and Spirit Voices

Spirit photography has been occurring since 1861, and now more than two dozen people in half a dozen countries have claimed to obtain pictures of a variety of types of images that seem to be permanently visible proof of an afterlife. Most of these cannot be adequately evaluated now, because the photographers are themselves dead. We have either to accept or reject the statements given by those connected with the incidents.

A Boston photographer, William Mumler, gave us the first photographic plate of an "extra," as they came to be called. He claimed to have discovered it on the plate after it was developed. No one noticed its presence while the shot was being taken, he said. Eventually Mumler was charged with swindling, but the trial acquitted him because in many instances it turned out that he had nothing to do with the spirit forms that showed up alongside the people he photographed. The relatives of the deceased told the court that they had no photographs or negatives of the ones who appeared on the exposed plates. Obviously, then, Mumler couldn't have faked the pictures.

Tape recordings from the dead is a recent discovery of a Swedish film producer, Friedrich Jurgenson. In the 1960s, he made some tapes of bird voices in the country, and found to his surprise that he could also hear a quiet male voice discussing bird songs in Norwegian. Jurgenson continued to investigate this phenomenon, and eventually extra voices began giving personal messages to him in the presence of witnesses.

These came to the attention of a Latvian psychologist, Dr. Konstantin Raudive. Raudive then amassed 70,000 voice effects recorded by microphone, radio, and various other devices specially constructed for him by interested electronics engineers. The voices are always faint, sometimes indistinct and hard to distinguish from background noise. But when recognizable, they are apparently human voices speaking in a mixture of languages, including Latvian, Swedish, German, Russian and English. The voice entities enter into conversation with Raudive and others, respond after being addressed, and give answers that are relevant, although some utterances seem inconsequential or nonsensical.

This phenomenon is the least verified of all those that make up the evidence for life after death, and there seems to be strong indication that some of the voices are spurious radio effects and possibly even psychokinetically-imprinted thoughts (mind over matter) originating from the experimenters rather than discarnate humans.

Perhaps the most unusual and promising form of electronic communication with the dead is the work of Dr. George W. Meek of the Metascience Research Foundation in Franklin, North Carolina. After retiring from a long and distinguished career in engineering, Meek spent a decade, working in conjunction with many scientists and electronics experts around the world, to develop a device he calls Spiricom. The name is derived from "spirit communications." Meek claims the device allows communication with the dead and has eliminated the need for a human medium. He offers tape recordings purportedly of deceased people speaking through the Spiricom device, and he backs up his claim with documentation, full instructions and schematics by which others can build their own

Spiricom. The full story of Meek's pioneering, provocative work is told in *The Ghost of 29 Megacycles* by the noted author, John Fuller. Meek himself gives details in his excellent book, *After We Die, What Then?*

Possession Cases

When the word *possession* is mentioned, most people probably think of *The Exorcist* and cackling demons. There are a number of interesting cases indicative of demonic possession, but there are others—the ones we're concerned with here—that appear to be due to the spirit of a deceased human rather than a nonhuman entity.

One such case, presented in Nils Jacobson's *Life After Death?*, was reported by the American minister and psychologist, Dr. Walter Franklin Prince. In 1922 he was consulted by a Mrs. Latimer, who begged him for help because she was convinced that the spirit of her male cousin, Marvin, was plaguing her. Marvin had died two years earlier. A day or so after his death, Mrs. Latimer began to hear a voice that sounded like his speaking to her hatefully. This voice was an inner one for her, and it made her life unbearable, saying, "You made me suffer and I will make you suffer."

Mrs. Latimer couldn't understand this so she asked the voice for an explanation. She was told that just before he died, Marvin had seen Mrs. Latimer writing a letter that contained a remark about him—a remark that had hurt his feelings profoundly. The spirit explained that he wouldn't stop tormenting her until she mentally apologized. Mrs. Latimer felt that in good conscience she could not apologize, so the torments continued.

When Mrs. Latimer sought help from Prince, he decided to attempt a different kind of treatment, because her case was so unlike anything that could be treated in a conventional manner. His approach was to assume that a spirit was present and to converse with the spirit through Mrs. Latimer. In effect, he used weighty arguments, an appeal to higher values and emotional persuasion on the spirit. He asked it to make an experiment of a few days in which he forgave Mrs. Latimer. Then the spirit was to see if he felt any better himself.

The experiment succeeded. The voice did not bother Mrs. Latimer again, and after several weeks she felt well enough to address the spirit herself.

"I shall not ask you to listen long," the voice said, "nor shall I ask you to hear me often hereafter. I am going away. But before I go, I want you to understand better what happened to you."

The voice described how he had died with embittered thoughts toward Mrs. Latimer, and how he could not free himself from them after death. He explained, "And after that, it was not I alone who molested you. Others grouped themselves around me, joined their efforts to mine, and urged me on. But I took the advice given me"—this referred to Prince's experiment—"sought the aid of those who were wise and good, and became free. And now I shall soon be gone away." The torment never returned and Mrs. Latimer was restored to vitality.

Deathbed Observations

Dr. Karlis Osis of the American Society for Psychical Research conducted several studies of the dying, based on observations made by almost 1800 doctors and nurses present during the last hours of terminal patients who were conscious to the end. These studies were made in the United States and India from 1960 to 1974. After the data were collected by questionnaire and personal interviews, they were fed to a computer for the first stage of analysis. The findings were printed and then analyzed by Osis and his colleague in the research, Dr. Erlendur Haraldsson. The men recently published a full report on their work in a book entitled *At the Hour of Death*.

India was chosen because of the great contrast between it and American culture. In India, where reincarnation is an accepted idea, a negative value is placed on preserving individuality after death. The Hindu goal is to get off the wheel of death and rebirth. Americans generally don't want that. We tend to have a keen sense of individuality and a wish to survive as personality. So if evidence of personal survival were found in India, the reasonable assumption is that it's not due to culturally conditioned factors.

What did Osis and Haraldsson find? Here's the way Osis put it to me:

> The experiences of the dying are basically the same, regardless of culture, education, sex or belief system, and their experiences cluster around something that makes sense in terms of survival after death, and a social structure to that afterlife.

He went on to specify the findings of this monumental study, which is the first truly scientific examination of this category of survival evidence. I will quote from my interview:

> We found that the dying went through some startling experiences—experiences that were not due to the patients' medical condition. For one thing, there were frequent instances of elevation in mood. I mean that the patients became happier at the very time when the doctor was usually saying conditions were desperate. They died with feelings of serenity, peace, elation, and religious emotions. And this mood change was not due to any medication, sedation, lack of oxygen to the brain, or the nature of the illness. The patients died a "good death" in strange contrast to the usual gloom and misery commonly expected before expiration.
>
> Another remarkable thing that terminal patients experienced was deathbed visions. These visions were of two kinds: one was where they would see a person or a religious apparition—a hallucination that no one else could see. An invisible visitor would come into the hospital and the patient would talk with it. Usually, it was a close relative or friend, but it might also be a religious or mythological figure such as Jesus or Krishna. The doctors and nurses knew of these apparitions only because the patient talked about them.

The other kind of visionary experience was where the patient saw surroundings as if it were another place, another reality. You could call these scenes nonhuman nature. Again, only the dying saw them. In almost every case, whether it was a figure or a landscape, the visions were of a positive sort. The hell-and-brimstone sort of place simply didn't appear.

In these studies care was taken to see if the hallucinations were due to expectation, wish fulfilment, belief, worry, mood, or some normal factor, including, as mentioned, the patient's medical condition. Osis and Haraldsson found that these were not the cause. The experiences were generally the same in both cultures, and show that the information from the dying is consistent across cultures with the idea of life after death.

Another kind of deathbed observation involves careful weighing of dying persons. The first study was made in 1907 by a Harvard psychologist, Dr. William McDougall. He found an inexplicable sudden weight loss of about an ounce at the moment of expiration. Recently, a doctor in England and another in West Germany made the same observation. The weight loss, they said, could not be explained anatomically or physiologically. Apparently something leaves the body quite suddenly at the moment of death—something which weighs more than the air normally in the lungs.

That something may have been photographed by a Frenchman named Baraduc at the beginning of this century. He made several photographs of his dying son, and six months later when his wife passed on, he did the same for her. In both instances Baraduc's photographs show a cloud-like substance concentrated a little way above the dying body. These photos have never been explained away by parapsychologists or skeptics.

Near-Death Experiences

This term refers to an experience in which a person is clinically dead but is somehow resuscitated. All vital signs are missing in the person—no breath, no heartbeat, no brainwaves. There have been many such cases recorded, with some people dead for up to half an hour. Of interest to us here is a special subgroup—those who claim to have been conscious throughout their death experience and who remembered what went on.

Many people who suffer clinical death have no memory at all of what transpired while they were dead. But those who do have sometimes startled their onlookers by reporting the exact details of what was said and done by them. A typical case would be someone who dies on the operating table. While the doctors are frantically working, and telling the nurses and other staff to do things, the "dead" person experiences himself as being outside his body, floating in air near the ceiling, invisibly observing and hearing with clear perception.

This sort of experience is amazing in itself, but there's more to it. The "dead" would have a most interesting story to tell, and researchers have begun to gather the details in a comprehensive way. Kübler-Ross claims to have talked with more than 1,000 such people. But the best-known source of information on near-death experiences is Moody's *Life After Life*. Moody compiled his accounts into a composite profile of the near-death experience which goes like this:

> A man is dying and, as he reaches the point of greatest physical distress, he hears himself pronounced dead by the doctor. He begins to hear an uncomfortable noise, a loud ringing or buzzing, and at the same time feels himself moving very rapidly outside his own physical body, but still in the same immediate physical environment, and sees his own body from a distance as though he is a spectator. He watches the resuscitation attempt from this vantage point and is in a state of emotional upheaval.
>
> After a while, he collects himself and becomes more accustomed to his odd condition. He notices that he still has a "body," but one of a very different nature and with very different powers from the physical body he has left behind. Some other things begin to happen. Others come

to meet him and help him. He glimpses the spirits of relatives and friends who have already died, and a loving, warm spirit of a kind he has never encountered before—a being of light—appears before him. This being asks him a question, nonverbally, to make him evaluate his life and helps him along by showing him a panoramic, instantaneous playback of the major events of his life. At some point, he finds himself approaching some sort of barrier or border, apparently representing the limit between earthly life and the next life. Yet, he finds that he must go back to the earth, that the time for his death has not yet come. At this point he resists, for by now he is taken up with his experiences in the afterlife and does not want to return. He is overwhelmed by intense feelings of joy, love, and peace. Despite his attitude, though, he somehow reunites with his physical body and lives.

Later he tries to tell others, but he has trouble doing so. In the first place, he can find no human words to describe these unearthly episodes. He also finds that others scoff, so he stops telling other people. Still, the experience affects his life profoundly, especially his views about death and its relationship to life.

Moody stresses that this is a prototype of the near-death experience and that not everyone he spoke to had every element of this composite picture. In all, there are eleven elements to it. First is its ineffability. Then comes hearing the news of one's own death, feelings of peace and quiet, the strange noise, the dark tunnel, finding oneself out of the body, meeting deceased humans, then meeting a being of light, and finally, the panoramic life review, the border between life and death, and coming back to life.

In a sequel entitled *Reflections on Life After Life*, Moody described four more elements of the near-death experience which a few people had mentioned to him. These are: a vision of knowledge in which past, present and future seem to co-exist in a timeless state; cities of light or heavenly dwelling places; a realm of bewildered spirits apparently "trapped" in a most unfortunate state of existence; and supernatural rescues from physical death by the action of some spiritual agent or being.

Moody found that the experiences his interviewees had not only convinced them of the reality of life after death, they also convinced Moody himself. Still, personal conviction is not the same as public demonstration, and Moody's reports were not what scientists would consider hard data. His books aroused much interest in this subject, but most researchers felt that more rigorous study was needed. One such person was Dr. Kenneth Ring of the psychology department at the University of Connecticut. In 1977, he and some colleagues began a two-year study of the near-death experience. The results were published in Ring's *Life at Death*.

In general, Ring's study confirms the main findings of Moody, but there are some differences also, though they're relatively minor. Most important of all, Ring's study is the first investigation devoted solely to near-death experiences which used scientific techniques in conducting the interviews and recording the results. Ring systematized the interviews so that information could be statistically analyzed and judgments made based on numerical data.

Ring's study is based on 102 interviews. He identified the people through referrals by hospital physicians, by writing to many psychiatrists and by advertising in Connecticut newspapers. About half of the 102 respondents nearly died from illness. The other half was evenly divided between accident and suicide cases. A little more than half the people were female. Most of the 102 were white and about half were married. Their religious affiliation was mostly Catholic and Protestant, though a few were Jewish and some were agnostic or atheist. They ranged in age from 18 to 84. Their average age at the time of their near-death was about 38, and most were interviewed within two years of their experience.

Ring, like Moody, found that a multi-stage process emerged from his data. In Ring's view, there are five stages in what he calls the "core experience" of the near-death process. Stage 1 is characterized by a feeling of peace and well-being. In Stage 2, there is a sense of separation from the body and then leaving it behind as a journey begins. Next, the person enters a transitional space which is completely black or dark, very peaceful, and usually without dimension. People float or drift through it into Stage 4, in which they see light appear—brilliant golden light. Finally, in Stage 5, they enter the light, where they sense themselves to be in another world of unforgettable, extraordinary beauty. There may be lovely gardens and landscapes; there may be ethereal music; there may be a reunion with deceased loved ones—relatives or friends.

Cross-cutting the intermediate stages is a decisional process in which the apparently dead person has some sort of life review or a conversation with the sensed divine presence. The decision is made to return to life, and the next thing the person knows is that he's awake, back in the body.

Ring found that not everyone goes through all these stages. Moreover, each stage can take a variety of forms. There isn't a rigid formula that must be followed. These experiences were *not* affected by an individual's age, sex, race, education, religion or prior degree of religiousness (skeptics and atheists recounted the same kinds of experiences as did devout believers). Apparently, also, it doesn't make much difference how you nearly die, except in the case of suicides, who tended to have far fewer and far less complete core experiences. No one in any category reported experiences which were predominantly unpleasant or hellish.

The aftereffects of the near-death experience are striking. In general, there is a marked shift in values toward the spiritual, and the total effect is akin to a spiritual rebirth. Most often people say they completely lose their fear of death, knowing it to be based on an illusion. They also find that they are more alive, more aware, more sensitive to beauty in the natural world and to the feelings of others. They tend to become stronger psychologically and to have a greater sense of self-worth. They also feel strongly a need to be of service to society in some way, as if they now have a purpose for being in the world—a purpose that came clear to them only through the near-death experience. They are more willing and able to express love and concern to others, and they're more tolerant of others. Their religious sense is deepened, not especially by going to church or temple so much as by a constant background feeling of a spiritual dimension underpinning life. They have an inward feeling of closeness to God and to their fellow man. Altogether, they tend to express thanks for having had the near-death experience.

The Meaning of Life After Death

Now that we've looked at the evidence for life after death, we can ask ourselves: What does it mean for us? As I said at the beginning of this chapter, we're now in a position to say *there is a rational basis for religious faith.* All the world's major religions and spiritual traditions, from ancient times to the present, maintain that human existence does not end with death. Some see consciousness continuing in personal forms; some see consciousness reuniting with a cosmic intelligence or universal soul. And some see both happening through a continued process of spiritual evolution.

The foundation of these traditions is the mystical experience. That is an experience in which knowledge of our cosmic origin and destiny is obtained directly through insight or revelation or enlightenment, rather than through intellectual analysis or philosophic reasoning. One of the best-known writers on mystical experience was the Canadian psychiatrist, R.M. Bucke. In his classic book, *Cosmic Consciousness*, he noted that hundreds of historical figures who had experienced cosmic consciousness were unanimous in saying that with mystical illumination the fear of death which haunts so many people "falls off like an old cloak." He adds that this is not a result of reasoning—the fear simply vanishes. It vanishes because they saw that death was an illusion, something they'd been tricked into thinking or conditioned into believing by the world. The enlightened person knows that the universe is not a dead machine, not a lifeless mechanical process, not a threatening conspiracy to swallow up people into annihilation. Rather, Bucke remarks, the universe is a "living presence" and the enlightened person experiences this directly, thereby knowing that existence continues beyond what is called death.

We will look at the nature of the mystical experience more closely later on because there is much to be gained in just study *about* it, even if you don't have the mystical experience yourself. For the moment consider this: from the point of view of mystics, death is a transition, not a termination. It is an adventure in consciousness—the beginning of a further state of development in the continuum of consciousness stretching from the inorganic world to the cosmic intelligence which created it, God.

Now, I am not saying that the evidence for life after death supports any particular religious doctrine or institution. There is definitely a cultural overlay on our popularized versions of the afterlife experience, and we'll look more closely at that in Chapter 17. But whether it is seen in personal terms or transpersonal terms, whether it is heaven or *nirvana* or the Happy Hunting Ground or the Garden of Paradise, the weight and authority of tradition maintains that death is just an alteration in our state of consciousness, and that the quality of our continued existence in the afterlife depends on the quality of our living here and now. In other words, post-mortem life reflects the degree to which we have evolved in consciousness and grown in spiritual awareness.

Equally important, the experience of the mystics shows that we do not have to wait for physical death to enter into eternal life. Rather—and this is quite paradoxical— immortality is ours *already* and we can realize it *now*, in the flesh, the moment we are born again into the spirit, the living eternal spirit of the cosmos. I am not talking about physical immortality at this point, though I will later on. I am speaking about losing your fear of dying by understanding that death is not what you ordinarily think it is. I am speaking, in fact, about a change in your state of consciousness. And you can obtain this knowledge, this enlightenment, *now*, in this lifetime, and *that* is what truly and finally frees you from the deadening idea that you are only a body or—equally bad—only a pawn-like soul bound to a wheel of endless deaths and rebirths. It is paradoxical but nonetheless true, the mystics tell us, that genuine freedom from fear of dying is also genuine release from the cosmic process—*karma*, if you will—that requires rebirth or reincarnation.

We overcome our fear of dying by understanding the death experience—how and why we die. In this chapter I have tried to give you some theoretical knowledge and some scientific evidence to aid your understanding. I purposely placed this chapter here in order to give you some immediate hope and reassurance that death is not the end of you. But intellectually-grasped information needs to be complemented by experientially-realized direct knowledge. This deepens your understanding and makes it personally yours, based on first-hand experience as well as theory. In the following chapters we will do just that.

3
Admitting Your
Fear of Dying

Dag Hammarskjold, former Secretary-General of the United Nations, died in 1961 in a plane crash in Africa. We don't know what his last moments were like, but we can guess. When he was found, he had a fractured spine, broken ribs, a broken thigh and breastbone, and internal hemorrhaging. His hand clutched a tuft of grass but his face, according to a biography, was "extraordinarily peaceful." Hammarskjold was widely regarded as a spiritually-aware man. He once wrote, "No choice is uninfluenced by the way in which the personality regards its destiny, and the body its death. In the last analysis, it is our conception of death which decides our answers to all the questions that life puts to us ... hence, too, the necessity of preparing for it." Hammarskjold was prepared. Are you?

How do *you* regard your destiny? What is *your* attitude toward death? Are you *prepared* to die? Are your "affairs in order"—emotionally and spiritually, as well as legally and financially?

Most probably you have some abstract concept of death but it's something you've never examined closely because it seems terrifying. We're going to do that now. First we'll hear what two doctors have to say, because they are people who by training and experience ought to be able to offer us insight. In this instance, however, it turns out that both

29

doctors had not really come to intimate personal terms with death and dying. Their struggles to do so have real usefulness for you.

Dr. Julian Kirchick, who died in 1978, discovered at age 60 that he was terminally ill, and kept a journal of his final four years. He first became aware that he was dying by "seeing" an apparition of death personified. As he rested in his backyard one day, according to a *Newsday* reporter, who read Kirchick's journal,

> I was startled by a rustling in the bushes about 20 feet away. I rose from my chaise lounge to investigate. After taking about two steps, I suddenly stopped short. For there was a ghastly intruder, the face of Death. He was dressed in a monk-like robe with a large hood and large sleeves, which hung low. The tissue-like skin was drawn tautly against the skull. Eyes, which were absent from the sunken hollow-eye sockets, seemed to pierce my very soul. Strangely, the teeth parted in what appeared a friendly smile. His bony hand beckoned to me in a benign gesture. "Come to me," he seemed to say. My feet froze in my tracks. I was immobilized by a chilling fright which ran down my spine.

Hallucination or not, you'd expect that a doctor of 60 would have become more accustomed to death, wouldn't you? That's no disparagement of Kirchick, incidentally. His fear reaction is probably typical of medical people— *because* of their medical training! In *At the Hour of Death*, Osis and Haraldsson point out:

> Medical texts tell us in no uncertain terms that after the heart stops circulating blood, the brain is no longer nourished and begins to decay rapidly—within a quarter of an hour or so. At that point, the texts say, the patient's personality is simply no more. It is irreparably destroyed. The individual ceases to exist.
>
> For centuries, medical schools have inculcated this grim, uncompromising concept into doctors and nurses— those who will be the ones to help us when we die.

The experience of Dr. Sherman Hershfield confirms this. In a letter to columnist Jory Graham in early 1979,

Hershfield wrote of discovering his deep feelings about death—feelings that had been covered over by a veneer of "clinical objectivity" and "unemotional involvement with patients." He told how his best friend—a medical colleague —died, and how this forcibly directed him to pay attention to what he'd kept submerged for so long in order to conform to the medical image.

> Until four years ago, I never faced my own fears—I never knew I had them. Death was the last thing on my mind. Dying was dying, and I felt I knew everything there was to know about it. I was "taught everything" in medical school about death, at least that's what I'd been told. Looking back, I realize we were taught very little. . . .
>
> We physicians are an inadequate lot in facing our feelings about death and in helping our patients to handle theirs. We have so much to learn, but I do not know how we will unless we are able to admit our deepest fears to ourselves. It is a very complex problem and I do not know where the answers lie, only that the education in human values must begin in the medical schools. As for myself, I do not know all the answers to life, but I am trying to learn day by day.

This kind of honest and humble confession is the necessary first step toward relieving yourself of the burden that fear places on you. That is what I now want you to do. Find a place where you can be alone, and then get quiet within yourself. Relax your body. Still your mind. When you feel comfortable, take a breath and say aloud to yourself:

> *I admit, honestly and completely, that I am afraid of dying. I am not going to hide from the fact any more. I am going to face it as the first step toward conquering it.*

Say it slowly and with emphasis. Really listen to yourself. Feel the power of relief in your admission—a power that can change your life by honestly facing your fear.

To help you admit your fear even more freely, and to help you focus more clearly on exactly what it is about death that frightens you, I'd like you to take a very short and simple True/False test called the Death Anxiety

Scale (DAS). It was designed by a psychologist, Dr. Donald I. Templer, who published it in *The Journal of General Psychology* in April, 1970. The Death Anxiety Scale reflects a wide range of life experiences into which you may be projecting yourself and identifying yourself. There are no "right" and "wrong" answers to the test. Its purpose is to show you the general degree of your own anxiety about dying. I'll discuss your results afterward. Proceed now with the test.

Death Anxiety Scale

Circle T or F for your answer. T = true, F = false.

T   F   1.   I am very much afraid to die.

T   F   2.   The thought of death seldom enters my mind.

T   F   3.   It doesn't make me nervous when people talk about death.

T   F   4.   I dread to think about having to have an operation.

T   F   5.   I am not at all afraid to die.

T   F   6.   I am not particularly afraid of getting cancer.

T   F   7.   The thought of death never bothers me.

T   F   8.   I am often distressed by the way time flies so rapidly.

T   F   9.   I fear dying a painful death.

T   F   10.   The subject of life after death troubles me greatly.

T   F   11.   I am really scared of having a heart attack.

T   F   12.   I often think about how short life really is.

T   F   13.   I shudder when I hear people talking about World War III.

T F 14. The sight of a dead body is horrifying to me.

T F 15. I feel that the future holds nothing for me to fear.

To score yourself on the Death Anxiety Scale, remember that there are no absolute "right" and "wrong" answers. You are simply describing your own situation, which may be more or less anxious than another person's. According to Templer, six questions are keyed "False." These are 2, 3, 5, 6, 7 and 15. All the rest are keyed "True." Thus, a person can have a DAS score as high as 15, if he answers all the items in the keyed direction, or as low as 0, if none of the items are answered in the key direction.

As you will see in Chapter 11, however, there have been some rare individuals who are utterly unafraid of death and who could therefore have truthfully answered all fifteen questions opposite to what Templer suggests is a normal response. These people have been universally revered as saints and heroes, and should be thought of as models for you in your efforts to come to terms with personal death.

Templer does not give scoring directions in his article, nor a scale by which to evaluate your score. However, in a 1971 *Psychological Reports* article which he kindly brought to my attention, Templer noted that although no actual norms have been established for the Death Anxiety Scale, a considerable amount of relevant data has been collected. Normal subjects, he said, tend to score roughly from 4.5 to 7.0 on the range from 0 to 15, with standard deviations of 3.0 or so possible. "Psychiatric patients obtain higher scores than normals. Females consistently have higher DAS scores than males." Also, there seems to be no relationship between age and DAS scores. In general, about 2/3 of the general population score between 3 and 10.

According to one counselor whom I consulted on use of the DAS (because he includes it in a death awareness course he teaches), most people score about 60% of the questions in the direction of low death anxiety.

Although he was unaware of Templer's 1971 article, his

observations and Templer's are in approximate agreement. He also noted that individual scores may vary from the norm because the person may have just gone through a trying experience—such as an accident or the death of a loved one—which (like Dr. Hirshfield) forced him to be especially aware of death.

Therefore, I suggest this for scoring yourself. If your score is between three and ten in accordance with the True-False answers that Templer gives, you can consider yourself as being within the norm. Understand, however, that in this case "normal" doesn't mean "the most healthy condition." Ideally, you should score 0, indicating no anxiety whatsoever. Even the ideal score of 0 may be misleading, since it might mean that, rather than being free from death anxiety, you are strongly repressing awareness of death. Thus, a strong awareness of death, which is personally unacceptable, can be kept from consciousness through the defense mechanism of repression. This creates a cosmetic facade of fearlessness that falsely imitates the true condition of saints and heroes.

It is unhealthy, psychologists tell us, to repress or deny our awareness of death. But it is just as unhealthy to be so keenly conscious of it all the time that it interferes with daily living. In Chapter 1, I discussed briefly how denial and repression of death-fear is so pervasive. Here I'll mention those people at the other end of the scale who are overwhelmingly conscious of their mortality. *Everything* seems to threaten them, and they worry needlessly to the point of ill health, both physical and mental. They may, for example, develop some compulsive behavior that is really a disguised magical ritual for evading death. They may also have a recurring dream or dream imagery that disturbs sleep to the point of desperation. Some become hypochondriacs, seeing symptoms of illness in themselves and inventing new ones when medical diagnosis shows them to be free of that particular ailment. Others may develop phobias. In all cases, their functional ease and efficiency are reduced, often to the point of incapacity.

Your aim in dealing with fear of dying should be to

reduce it and its effects in your life, and eventually eliminate it altogether, so that death may occur to you at any time and you'll be ready for it in all respects. In such a state, daily existence becomes free, joyful, creative and of great value to others through your example and your service. In later chapters you will see how to prepare for death—physically, psychologically, socially, spiritually. In fact, you will see that it is actually possible to *laugh* at death! The next chapter will begin to show you how.

4

Laughing at Death

FUNKY WINKERBEAN · Tom Batiuk

Humor is a great tension reducer. By making light of our feelings, we can look more directly at a frightening situation and see it with greater detachment. It helps us to adjust to something we don't want to face. If we can laugh at it, there's hope for us! When the idea of death is met in a joke or humorous situation, its incongruity helps us to take both it and ourselves less somberly. Digger O'Dell the friendly undertaker and St. Peter at the pearly gates are familiar forms. So is gallows humor. Laughter raises our morale and restores us, even when confronted with— pardon the expression—such a grave situation as death. (That was a bad pun, perhaps, but I have Shakespeare to thank for the idea. In *Romeo and Juliet*, when witty

Funky Winkerbean by Tom Batiuk, ©1980 Field Enterprises, Inc. Courtesy of Field Newspaper Syndicate.

Mercutio is dying from a sword thrust, he jests, "Ask for me tomorrow and you'll find a grave man.")

In this short chapter, I hope you'll have a good laugh or two—at the expense of death and dying. We'll get more serious (but not somber) in the following chapters. Here, however, it seems appropriate to indulge in plain old hilarity—the sort you find in the rollicking Irish ballad about an alcoholic hodcarrier, Tim Finnegan. James Joyce's masterwork, *Finnegans Wake*—a mighty novel about the fall and redemption of humanity—is drawn from this comic tale.

Finnegan, it seems, had "a sort of tipplin' way." He'd been born with "the love of the liquor" and took "a drop" of it every morning before work. The word "whiskey," incidentally, comes from the ancient Gaelic *uisce* and means "water of life." It is ironic, therefore, that one day Finnegan, inebriated, fell from the ladder, broke his skull, and died. He was carried home, laid out upon the bed, and a wake began. His friends assembled, mourning him with whiskey punch. Soon an argument began between two mourners, which led to "a row and a ruction." The last verse of the song tells what must be called—this time without apologies—the punch line:

Then Micky Maloney raised his head,
When a noggin of whiskey flew at him,
It missed and falling on the bed,
The liquor scattered over Tim;
Bedad he revives, see how he rises,
And Timothy rising from the bed,
Says, "Whirl your liquor around like blazes,
Your souls from the devil, do ye think I'm dead?"

Did it at least get a smile from you? It reminds me of the Irishman attending his friend's wake who wanted to console the widow, but didn't know how. At last, after an awkward interval, he cleared his throat and said, "Terry looks a lot better since he stopped drinking."

Surely it was whiskey-soaked Irish wakes which inspired the doggerel verse:

Little Willie's dead.
Jam him in the coffin,
For you don't get the chance
Of a funeral often.

And speaking of coffins, did you smokers know, "It's not the cough that carries you off; it's the coffin they carry you off in"?

Coffins, of course, were the reason Digger O'Dell always bade people goodbye by saying, "Well, I've got to be shoveling off." But do you know why an undertaker is the most trustworthy person around? Because he's the last person in the world who'll ever let you down!

Did you hear about the undertaker who signed his letters, "Eventually yours"? He had a billboard in front that advertised, "You die—we do all the rest."

Then there's the guy who said on April 15, "Nothing's certain except death and taxes, and I wish they'd come in that order!"

Columnist Jim Bishop reports that his father, to break the tension surrounding the topic of death, wisecracked, "Personally, dying is something I've reserved as the last thing I want to do."

George Bernard Shaw, the Irish playwright, drolly declared that either he would live to be immortal or else die trying.

And did you know there are two conditions of seasickness? The first is when you're so sick that you're afraid you'll die. The second is when you're so sick that you're afraid you *won't* die!

The innocence and curiosity of children often provides humor based on death. Their lack of a strongly formed self-concept leads them to say things that strike us as funny because their comments are so contrary to our ideas and expectations. My first child, when she was barely four, was sitting beside me as we drove past a graveyard one day. She looked at it, thought for a moment, and then asked, "Daddy, is that where all the dead people live?"

Another young child, whose grandmother had just died, asked his mother where Grammy had gone. The mother

replied that she was in heaven. The next day, when the
family had gathered around the grave, the little boy looked
at the tombstones and lawn, and then piped up to his
mother, "Mommy, is this heaven?"

Yet another youngster was faced with the loss of a grand-
parent, and he, too, asked his mother what had happened.
"Your grandfather died and his soul went to heaven," the
mother answered. Looking at the body in the casket, the
little boy asked, "Then what's that—the leftovers?"

Those are all true stories, but "The Cremation of Sam
McGee" is a tall tale which has given a laugh to people
for many years. Sam, a gold prospector in the Yukon, hated
the constant Arctic cold and yearned for the balmy climate
of his native Tennessee. As he lay dying, he thought rue-
fully of being frozen forever in an icy grave and therefore
asked his partner to cremate, rather than bury, him. His
partner complied, using the boiler of an abandoned ship.
A huge fire was lit, and when the partner thought Sam's
body had been thoroughly burned, he looked inside
the boiler:

> And there sat Sam, looking cold and calm, in the heart of
> the furnace roar;
> And he wore a smile you could see a mile, and he said,
> "Please close the door!
> It's fine in here, but I greatly fear you'll let in the cold
> and storm—
> Since I left Plumtree, down in Tennessee, it's the first
> time I've been warm."

Humor is sometimes found on gravestones. A careless
race car driver who died in a crash chose this epitaph:
"Excuse my dust." Then there are these:

> Here lies Johnny Yeast.
> Pardon me for not rising.

> Stranger, regard this spot with gravity.
> Dentist Brown is filling his last cavity.

I suspect that Dentist Brown was a terribly hard-
working man who practiced his profession almost nonstop.

This illustrates the wisdom of the saying, "Death is nature's way of telling you to slow down."

When Henry David Thoreau, the author of *Walden*, was on his deathbed, his Aunt Louisa asked him if he had made his peace with God. Thoreau replied, "I did not know we had ever quarrelled, Aunt."

Another item in the Famous Last Words Department concerns the flamboyant British poet, Oscar Wilde. As he was taking his last breath, he noticed the curtains in his room with displeasure and murmured, "Either they go or I do."

There, now. You feel a little better, don't you? In the last chapter you admitted your fear of dying. Here you've just had a good chuckle from the very thing that seemed so frightening. Perhaps death is not cause for all the alarm you've felt. As we go on, you'll see exactly that. Meanwhile, ponder this little bit of wisdom based on mixing the dangers of alcohol with Thoreau's unflinching optimism. "Is life worth living? It depends on the liver!"

Death is like your shadow: always with you. No matter how hard you may run, you can't escape it. Some people are afraid of their own shadow, but you and I know that such a fear is irrational. By the same token, your fear of dying is like being scared of your own shadow. You've been telling yourself for a long time, perhaps unconsciously, that death is fearful. Now I'm telling you there's no reason to be afraid of death. Who's right?

To find out, you need direct experience. Logical argument will take us only so far. I could build a fine, logical argument but if it isn't based on valid premises and solid facts the argument is merely imagination, fantasy, or wishful thinking. Direct experience—short of actually dying, of course—is the best basis for judging whether my argument is both logical and true. It's also the best basis for judging whether your fear of death is as unjustified and unnecessary as being afraid of your own shadow.

In the following chapters, therefore, you're going to

"walk through the valley of the shadow of death" and find that the awful bogeyman is, in fact, a fantastically false argument that you were tricked into believing.

My thanks to Glenn M. Vernon for the chapter "Death and Humor" in his book, *Sociology of Death*, from which I adapted some of this material.

5
Dealing with the Pain of Dying

There is a story of a Zen master whose monastery and surrounding countryside were threatened by the savage destructiveness of a barbaric war lord. Everyone except the old Zen master fled. When the war lord heard that the old monk had not left, he was infuriated and came to confront the master. With drawn sword he said to the old man, "Why haven't you fled? Don't you know I can run you through with my sword without batting an eye?" The Zen master calmly replied, "Yes. But don't you know I can be run through with your sword without batting an eye?" It is reported that the war lord turned and left, humbled by the Zen master's serenity in the face of death.

I've already explained *how* people come to fear death—by using their unique human capacity to anticipate the future and project themselves into it. This allows them to foresee various circumstances that appear entirely unpleasant. But that doesn't sufficiently explain *why* they fear it. We'll look at the *why* throughout the book and especially in the last chapter. Here we'll consider the *what.*

There are, in my judgment, five principal aspects to the fear of dying. They are:

1. Fear of pain—i.e., torture to the physical body.
2. Fear of loss—i.e., both separation from loved ones and companions, and loss of one's faculties.

3. Fear of meaninglessness—i.e., not being needed and loved any more, and therefore having been a failure.
4. Fear of the unknown—i.e., journeying into the unfamiliar, often with a sense of foreboding about eternal damnation and punishment for sinful behavior.
5. Fear of nonbeing—i.e., self-annihilation or the total disappearance of your identity.

We've already seen evidence in Chapter 2 that your personality survives death, and survives it with a capacity for memory, feeling, perception, learning, and judgment. The evidence, I think, is enough to convince any rational person. The trouble is, fear of death is not rational—it's emotional, and emotions aren't so easily changed by logic and information. These are necessary, but it also takes more emotional experience to supercede the emotions that are draining you of vitality and joy. You'll get that later on. First, however, it is necessry to look at the facts about our fear of pain, which is the initial aspect of fear of dying. We fear pain, especially protracted, lingering pain. Death, it seems, is the most painful experience imaginable, and no one but a masochist likes pain, right? To die suddenly or in your sleep is, many say, the best way to go. At least you don't feel any pain.

Is there anything reasonable to say in response to this? Yes, there is. I don't disagree with it. I'd simply like to point out that pain is to some extent *a matter of choice*, and much of what we consider painful is so because we've been socially conditioned into it.

Consciousness research shows that humans have a marvelous capacity to modify their nervous system and, hence, their pain threshold. Yogis, for example, have demonstrated total insensibility to pain. You've probably seen pictures of fakirs sitting on their beds of nails. Firewalkers tread on red-hot coals. Komar the Hindu Fakir (who is really Vernon Craig of Ohio) holds the world record for firewalking—measured at more than 1200°! Jack Schwartz, a psychic, healer, and teacher in Washington, has shown many times before medical and scientific audiences that he can push a thick sailmaker's needle through his bicep without feeling the slightest bit of pain, yet his nervous system is no different from yours or mine. He's learned to control it, that's all. Brainwave measurements made on him at the time he pierced his arm showed that he was producing pure alpha waves—the brainwaves associated with peaceful, relaxed states of mind.

The accomplishments of yogis, firewalkers, and others like Jack Schwartz are not beyond your own capacity. Hyponotists can take an ordinary person and, through hypnosis, have him perform in a most extraordinary way. It is well known that hypnosis can produce selective anesthesia. Hypnotic subjects have been told that they will not feel a thing when a hot piece of glass or a flame touches their skin—and they've done just that! Their skin did not burn and they did not feel any pain, although ordinarily they would have.

Another thing to consider about pain can be seen in a comment by Ramana Maharshi, a great Indian saint who died of cancer in 1950. Some disciples thought that Maharshi had, in his consciousness, separated himself from his body and hence did not feel the pain of his flesh being eaten away.

"Perhaps you don't feel the pain?" one asked.

Maharshi replied, "There is pain, but there is no suffering."

This is a very important point that Maharshi made—an important lesson for us: pain is physical but suffering is psychological. Suffering is *fearful anticipation* of pain. Eliminate the fear and there is no suffering. There *may* be pain. After all, pain serves a useful biological purpose. As one writer puts it, it serves a "brilliant function" by warning us of life-threatening circumstances. But once we are warned and are aware of the circumstances, pain is to a large degree a matter of our choice.

It follows, therefore, that insofar as you do not fearfully anticipate pain, you will not suffer, even when dying. That realization should become self-reinforcing. First, you realize that pain and suffering are not inevitable, which is a relief in itself. Next, you realize that this part of your fear of dying is therefore irrational and unrealistic, which in turn leads to a reduction of your generalized fear of dying. When you add this insight to your previous one—the understanding that your personality survives death—you have already gone a long way toward relieving yourself of some heavy emotional baggage.

If you want to develop your ability to control pain, there are a lot of resources available. Bookstores have titles on self-hypnosis such as Freda Morris's *Self-Hypnosis in Two Days* or Melvin Power's *Hypnosis Self-Taught* and Komar's *Life Without Pain*. Jack Schwartz also gives instruction in his book, *Voluntary Controls*. In addition, there are cassette tape recordings and records that claim to teach self-hypnosis. You can find them listed in magazines such as *Psychology Today, Saturday Review,* and *Science Digest*. You can also get instruction from hypnotherapists; look in the yellow pages of your telephone directory or inquire through local doctors and psychiatrists. Even the American Cancer Society endorses the idea. In an article in the September 1985 issue of *CA: A Journal for Clinicians*, Dr. David Spiegel of Stanford University states that many patients with cancer can eliminate or reduce their need for pain-killing drugs if they learn to use mental skills, which are latent in most people, and he explains how he uses hypnotic techniques to treat cancer pain.

Last of all, various "mind control" courses such as Silva Mind Control and Alpha Dynamics include pain control as part of their curriculum. You should be aware, however, that these courses have had some justified criticism because the instructors are not in all cases well-qualified to lead you in the varied mental exercises they offer. In short, be courageous in your approach to conquering this fear, but not foolhardy. A sensible caution should be used in the matter of choosing a hypnotherapist or similar instructor.

The last thing to consider in dealing with fear of pain is the easy availability of pain-relieving drugs. This is a controversial subject in some quarters because our legal climate opposes it and because medical people are quite rightly concerned not to inadvertently create addicts.

However, there is a growing view among those who work with the dying that it's just plain silly to worry about terminal patients becoming addicted. The benefits outweigh the disadvantages by far, they say. In fact, the effects of various drugs are known with such precision that it is possible to prescribe medications that effectively block pain while leaving the patient relatively unaffected in consciousness. St. Christopher's Hospice, a facility for the terminally ill outside London, uses a blend of pain-relieving ingredients, one of which is heroin. Consequently, the patient is kept pain-free and at the same time, mentally alert to interact with others. This treatment is becoming available here also.

Do you still think your fear of pain is justified?

6

Saying Goodbye to Your Body

For ten minutes I was laughing out of control as I saw that part of my body is always dying. What is there to fear? Life and death are simultaneous. 2,500,000 red cells are being born and consumed every second! We are living flames, burning at the edge of this incredible joy.

Michael Murphy, *Jacob Atabet*

It would probably shock you to see a yogi sitting in meditation near a corpse, or smeared all over with ashes from a crematorium, but in India these are common practices by which some yogis achieve freedom from fear of dying. Moreover, some learn precise yogic techniques for dying painlessly, consciously and voluntarily. Swami Rama, who is perhaps the best-known yogi in America because of his remarkable feats of physiological control performed under scientific observation in various laboratories, writes:

> In the ancient yogic scriptures, it is said that there is a definite way of leaving the body. Eleven gates are described through which the *pranas* or subtle energy can exit. The yogi learns to leave through the gate called *Brahma Rundhra*, located at the fontanelle, the crown of the head. It is said that he who travels through this gate remains conscious and knows about life hereafter exactly as he knows life here.

47

This quotation comes from a book by Swami Rama, *Living with the Himalayan Masters.*° One chapter has some particularly useful information for those afraid of dying. In "The Techniques of Casting Off the Body," Rama describes how and why yogis voluntarily die.

> The techniques of dying which are used by yogis are very methodical, painless and conscious. This is unusual in the Western world, but not in the Himalayas. It is not like committing suicide, but is an exact process or way of leaving that body which is no longer an instrument for enlightenment. Such a body is considered to be a burden— an obstacle which might obstruct the journey of the dying man when he goes through his vast unconscious reservoir of memories. Only those who are not competent in higher techniques and not self-reliant on their yogic will power and control accept the normal methods of dying, which are definitely inferior to the yogic methods.

Lest you think this morbid, Rama explains elsewhere in the book that from the yogic point of view, death is a habit of the body, a necessary change. The dying man, he says, should be educated psychologically for this moment. Why? "The ... change called death is itself not painful, but the fear of death creates miseries for the dying man." Modern people, Rama writes, should explore yogic ways of gaining freedom from that fear which is called death.

We are not going to learn in a single chapter what it takes a yogi long and arduous training to learn, although I will mention briefly two of the yogic methods Rama describes for "casting off the body." One which is traditional to certain Himalayan yogis is to seat yourself in meditation, enter the state of consciousness called *samadhi*, and then allow the body to freeze in the cold mountain air. Another technique—very rare—involves meditating on the solar plexus in a certain way that generates great internal heat, inducing spontaneous combustion of the body. It then burns to ashes in a very short time.

°Available from the Himalayan International Institute, RD 1, Honesdale, PA 18431. Ask for the literature catalog.

Preliminary to learning how to cast off the body, a yogi trains himself to be aware that he is more than simply a body. This kind of training is used in other spiritual traditions also, as we will see in later chapters. Even among Eskimos, according to the Arctic explorer Rasmussen, the shamans (priests or medicine men) have an important training exercise in which they visualize their bodies divested of flesh and blood so that nothing remains but their bones.

> And [the shaman] must then name all the parts of his body, mentioning every single bone by name; and in so doing, he must not use ordinary speech, but only the special and sacred shaman's language which he has learned from his instructor. By thus seeing himself naked, altogether freed from the perishable and transient flesh and blood, he consecrates himself, in the sacred tongue of the shamans, to his great task. . . .

The experience underlying this technique has been spontaneously discovered time and again by people in all cultures throughout history. Through the power of consciousness they have learned that their existence is not limited to the body and that there are transcendent dimensions to life. Two examples of this follow. The first comes from the life of Ramana Maharshi, whom I mentioned earlier. In a book about Maharshi called *Self Realization: Life and Teachings of Sri Ramana Maharshi*, by B.V. Narasimha Swami, this account of Maharshi's encounter with death-fear is given as Maharshi himself told it.

> On that day as I sat alone there was nothing wrong with my health. But a sudden and unmistakable fear of death seized me. I felt I was going to die. Why I should have so felt cannot now be explained by anything felt in my body. Nor could I explain it to myself then. I did not, however, trouble myself to discover if the fear was well grounded. I felt, "I am going to die," and at once set about thinking out what I should do. I did not care to consult doctors or elders or even friends. I felt I had to solve the problem myself then and there.
>
> The shock of fear of death made me at once introspective, or "introverted." I said to myself mentally—i.e., without

uttering the words—"Now, death has come. What does it
mean? What is it that is dying? This body dies." I at once
dramatized the scene of death. I extended my limbs and
held them rigid as though *rigor mortis* had set in. I imitated
a corpse to lend an air of reality to my further investigation.
I held my breath and kept my mouth closed, pressing the
lips tightly together so that no sound might escape. Let
not the word "I" or any other word be uttered! "Well then,"
said I to myself, "this body is dead. It will be carried stiff
to the burning ground and there burnt and reduced to
ashes. But with the death of this body, am 'I' dead? Is the
body 'I'? This body is silent and inert. But I feel the full
force of my personality and even the sound 'I' within
myself—apart from the body. So 'I' am a thing transcending
the body. The material body dies, but the spirit transcending it cannot be touched by death. I am therefore the
deathless spirit." All this was not a mere intellectual
process, but flashed before me vividly as living truth, something which I perceived immediately without any argument
almost. "I" was something very real, the only real thing in
that state, and all the conscious activity that was connected
with my body was centered on that. The "I" or my "self"
was holding the focus of attention by a powerful fascination
from that time forward. Fear of death had vanished at once
and forever. Absorption in the self has continued from
that moment right up to this time.

A contemporary American spiritual teacher Da Free
John had a parallel experience. In his autobiography,
The Knee of Listening,° he reports how he, too, overcame
the fear of death by "dying." Like Maharshi, when his fear
of death became almost overwhelming, he discovered
the ancient wisdom of giving in (which is quite different
from giving up) and cooperating with the process, flowing
with the pressure, letting "death" take its full and natural
course. Here's what happened in Da Free John's case.

°Available from the Dawn Horse Book Depot, P.O. Box 3680,
Clearlake Highlands, CA 95422. Ask for the literature catalog.
  Previous to September, 1979, Da Free John was known as
Bubba Free John. *The Knee of Listening*, published in 1973, lists
Bubba Free John as author. He is now Da Love-Ananda.

All day I stretched alone on the floor of the living room, revolving in this same overwhelming fear of death.

When Nina came home she tried to make me comfortable, and I passed the evening in front of the TV set, observing my terror.

When Nina went to bed I also tried to sleep. But the fever of the experience only increased. Finally, I woke her in the middle of the night and asked her to take me to the hospital. My breathing had become alarming, and my heart seemed to be slowing down. At times my heart would beat irregularly and seem to stop.

She drove me to a nearby emergency ward. I was examined by a nurse, and then a psychiatrist, who told me I was having an anxiety attack. There was nothing apparently wrong with me physically. He gave me a sleeping pill and told me to rest. If I felt no relief within a couple of days, I should seek psychiatric help.

Finally, on the third day after this process began, I was lying home alone in the afternoon. It was as if all my life had constantly prevented this experience from going to its end. All my life I had been preventing my death.

I lay on the floor, totally disarmed, unable to make a gesture that could prevent the rising fear. And thus it grew in me, but, for the first time, I allowed it to happen. I could not prevent it. The fear and the death rose and became my overwhelming experience. And I witnessed the crisis of that fear in a moment of conscious, voluntary death. I allowed the death to happen, and I saw it happen.

When that moment of crisis passed I felt a marvelous relief. The death had occurred, but I had observed it! I remained untouched by it. The body and the mind and the personality had died, but I remained as an essential and unqualified consciousness.

When all of the fear and dying had become a matter of course, when the body, the mind and the person with which I identified myself had died, and my attention was no longer fixed in those things, I perceived or enjoyed reality, fully and directly. There was an infinite bliss of being, an untouched, unborn sublimity, without separation, without individuation, without a thing from which to be separated. There was only reality itself, the incomparable nature and constant existence that underlies the entire adventure of life.

I think you'll agree that these anecdotes are most interesting and instructive. But you'll also agree that someone else's experience is not your own. Just as you'd rather actually eat a gourmet meal than look at a picture of one, when it comes to conquering your fear of death, no one else can do it for you. There is no substitute for direct experience. You have to do it yourself.

Bodies are wondrous creations—temples for the spirit—and not to be disdained or mistreated. Someday, however, you will have to give up your attachment to the body—that is, your self-identification with it. In this chapter, therefore, you will, like a yogi, use your power of visualization to become accustomed to the idea that someday your body will die and decay. You will learn to accept death as a fact, and you will see that your emotional response to that fact is something quite separable from it. There is a saying that applies here: If you can't change your fate, change your attitude. In other words, *accept* your death rather than deny it because that acceptance—that change of attitude—is what will free you from fear of death.

Here's what you will do in this exercise, which I call "The Way of All Flesh." You are going to read aloud to yourself a particularly vivid description of what happens to an organism at the time of death. The description tells how a body decomposes. If you are squeamish, be prepared for a mental shock. The point is to de-condition yourself, to break down the false identity you have made of being simply a body. You will also begin to break the emotional response that you've been conditioned into automatically producing at the idea of death.

You see, even though you may be able to control pain, if you conceive of yourself as *only* a body, then of course it is logical to think that the essence of you will disappear at death. This disidentification exercise, if done with real force of imagination, will help to support your intellectual knowledge of life beyond death by *emotionally* overriding your attachment to the body that you think is the whole of you.

The following passage comes from the opening pages of

Robert Payne's *The Corrupt Society*. It may terrify you or
revolt you at first, but if so, since you are by yourself for
this exercise, simply put the book down and sit quietly
until you have composed yourself. Then go back to the
beginning of the passage and start reading it again until
you can read it through completely. I've adapted this from
a Buddhist practice in which the student meditates in a
graveyard. After becoming acutely aware of all the decaying
flesh in the environment, he is instructed to contemplate
his own inevitable decomposition.

Now *you* will also. As you read, imagine that the decomposing body is *you*. Mentally project yourself into the
scene. *Feel* it happening in your own body. *See* your body
in those circumstances. Say to yourself, *This is me. This is
how I will be someday. I accept it. I accept without reserva-
tion that it is to be my fate. I am willing to die. I am willing
to die because I am more than a body. I will survive the
death of my body.*

Repeat this exercise as often as necessary to be able to
go through it without an overwhelming emotional response
of fear or revulsion. Your goal is peace of mind, serenity—
even in the face of death. As I said, you may not be able
to change your fate (although the immortalists disagree),
but you can change your attitude. And therein, paradoxically, is the key to conquering death by conquering
fear of death. Now begin.

> When a man dies, strange things happen to him. But they
> happen in an orderly fashion, logically, according to
> scientific laws. The processes leading to birth require
> only nine months, but the processes of corruption, the
> processes by which he is withdrawn from any semblance of
> life, cover a much longer span of time.
>
> All living creatures die, and the processes of corruption
> are very similar whether it is a man, an elephant, a tiger, a
> cat, or an insect. Death jolts the machine in a new and
> hitherto unsuspected direction, for which the body is
> ill-prepared and incapable of any resistance. Where
> previously there existed an intricate mechanism to sustain
> life, to move, to see, to understand, to adapt itself to its
> environment, there now takes place an irreversible

disintegration of the mechanism. The processes of corruption do not act evenly. Each part of the body has its own timetable, and some parts of the body function mechanically long after death has taken place.

The dead body remains active, but it is in a state of passive activity. Things are happening within it, but they are not things over which the body has any control. It suffers these things to happen to it; it has become finally a creature of necessity, at the mercy of forces incomparably stronger than itself.

Significantly, corruption sets in first at the top. The brain cells are alive for only four minutes after the heart has stopped beating. Even though the heartbeat may be revived, the infinitely complex machinery of the brain begins to be dismantled within four minutes, and there exists no medicine capable of reviving the dead brain. The heart is more enduring than the brain, for the auricles continue to contract even when the ventricles have already ceased beating. Thus, the right auricle is called *ultimum moriens*, the last to die.

In this way, according to varying timetables, the body gradually enters a state of corruption. While the brain dies almost immediately, the stomach continues to digest food for twenty-four hours after the heart has stopped beating. The digestion of food is completely purposeless; intended to sustain life, it becomes after death merely the continuation of an autonomous action never controlled by the brain. These independent organisms continue to flourish; the hair, fingernails and toenails continue to grow. The blood, too, retains its life-sustaining properties and remains liquid in the veins for hours after death. A leg or an arm severed or torn from the living body and therefore to all outward appearances dead can be joined to the body if the operation takes place within two hours. The dead limb is resurrected, feels pain, cold, heat, touch, glows with health. What is dead becomes alive because it can be knit into the living organism.

At death the arteries empty themselves into the veins and capillaries, and the blood settles in the lowest part of the body by force of gravity. The strange pallor of the upturned face of a corpse is in stark contrast to the blood-red appearance of the back of the corpse when it is suddenly turned over.

Between two and six hours after death *rigor mortis* sets in, beginning with the head. Complex chemical processes in the nerves and muscles bring about an increasing rigor, but two or three days later the same processes bring about a softening of the body. *Rigor mortis* is thus a very temporary phenomenon.

The first visible signs of decomposition occur twenty-four to forty-eight hours after death with the appearance of greenish-blue discolorations of the veins and a diffused greenish-blue discoloration of the abdomen. Thereafter the processes of corruption begin to move rapidly. The stomach finally stops digesting food, putrifies; the gases swell and push up the flesh. About the same time the cornea becomes completely opaque. The semen dies. The temperature of the body is now the same as that of the surrounding air. In time the soft parts of the body will assume the texture of glutinous jelly, then powder. The essential framework, the skeleton, may survive for many thousands of years.

Left alone, left to rot, the physical body assumes savage colors, purple, red, and green, with strange yellows and liquescent blacks. The skin pulls back from the lips in the familiar sardonic grin of death. The bloated flesh erupts, while worms and maggots carve tunnels through it. The decomposing corpse is a spectacle of the purest horror, which seems to have been designed as an ultimate punishment, an act of accusation against the living flesh. A month after a man has died he is scarcely recognizable; he has become a monster. All, or nearly all, that was human in him has been effaced. The brilliantly constructed machine, trained to respond to millions of subtle stimuli, now responds to nothing at all, spills out gases, changes colors, and serves no purpose except to manure a field.

Now you have died—in imagination. Now you have said goodbye to your body. You have learned to accept death—*your* death—or at least you are beginning to learn acceptance. In the following chapters you will go through more exercises designed to accustom you to death and make it familiar rather than fearful. You will also see why I said death can be your best friend. To anticipate, I'll say briefly here that death serves a useful purpose by challenging you to *live*—fully, consciously, joyfully. Wouldn't you be grateful to a friend who does that for you? Death, you will see, is the challenge given to us by nature to examine the meaning of life—our own lives and life in general. The next exercise will have you do just that.

7
How Will You Be Remembered?—Writing Your Own Obituary

Some years ago I taught an introductory journalism course in college. One of the beginning exercises I assigned my students was to write their own obituaries. This was a startling assignment for many of them—which is exactly what I intended. My purpose was twofold. First, I wanted them to write in a specific form in order to begin training them to do more than the free-flowing essays, reports, and creative writing they'd had in other courses. Second, I wanted them to begin to consider deeply what their lives were all about, and how a career in journalism might fit into that. In other words, the obituary was more than just a writing assignment. It was also an attempt to have them clarify their values and personal philosophy by looking in a somewhat detached way at what their lives might amount to and how they might be reported at the end.

In order to have the assignment really engage them, I began a classroom discussion of how people—in this case, potential journalists—often have hidden assumptions, biases and prejudices that can subtly color and control the way an event is reported. I said to them, "All right, let's find out if you have any unconscious assumptions. I'm going to ask you all a question now, and I want you to answer it silently to yourselves. I'll ask a question in such a way that you can reply with a number—just a simple number. But that number may tell you a lot about yourself. OK? Here's the question, and I want you simply to observe the first number that comes into your mind—the very first— before you have time to think about it or make some rational calculation."

I paused, and I'm going to pause here also because I want you, too, to participate in this exercise. I want you to do what my journalism students did, which is to mentally reply to the question I'm going to ask, and simply observe the number that comes into your mind. So when you're quiet and settled within yourself, read the question. How old will you be when you die?

What figure came to mind? Was it less than 50? 60? 90? Perhaps you didn't get a number at all. If so, that's all right, and I'll now explain why. Let's say a person is 37 years old, and as he read the question, the figure 55 came to mind spontaneously. What might it mean?

There are a variety of interpretations, and what I'll say here is offered only for your consideration. I'm not saying that it's absolutely true in every case. Nevertheless, it seems to me that the main thing this example shows is *an unconscious assumption* about that person's lifespan which may be subtly influencing most of his thought and behavior—even to the point of cellular functioning and physiological health. For some reason the person has the idea buried deeply in his mind that he'll die when he's 55. Perhaps a parent died at that age, and the fact has become embedded in the person's unconscious because he so closely identified with the parent. Perhaps he has an image of "old age" that says it basically begins at 45 or 50.

In other words, our 37-year-old has been walking around for a while with an idea or image in his mind that is driving his thoughts, his activities, and possibly even his physical health. His life is being driven by an assumption he isn't even aware of, and this assumption can become a self-fulfilling prophecy. Both psychology and psychosomatic medicine tell us this often happens.

Yet it needn't. Who says that old age begins at 45 or 50?

In some culture old age is defined as that time when you can no longer put in a full day's work in the fields, and that, chronologically speaking, happens at about 80 or 90. In addition, who says that old age is so bad? Our 37-year-old has the idea as part of the basic image unconsciously governing his life, but really it's nothing more than a matter of cultural conditioning. In some societies, the older you get, the more respected you become. You're considered an elder—not just an old person—when you can no longer work, and you're given a place of honor at the head of the table. Your role of elder means that you're regarded as a repository of wisdom, and your advice is actively sought and followed.

In youth-crazy America, of course, the aged are more often than not shunned by sticking them into "old folks' homes." This is sad, but it's also entirely a matter of cultural relativity. It can be changed—and, in fact, it *is* being changed, as you'll see in Chapter 12. But our 37-year-old hasn't begun to realize any of this. He simply stumbles along unhappily through daily existence with certain culturally-conditioned ideas deeply embedded in his outlook on life, never aware as he grew up that his thought and behavior have been subtly molded by the prejudices of his parents, teachers, authority-figures, etc.

The importance of all this for you should be obvious. I cannot emphasize too strongly the fact attested to by all the psychological and sociological studies, namely, that fear of death and dying is to a large extent *learned*. It is in great part a *socially-conditioned* emotional response which we pick up at such a young age that we assume it to be a part of reality. What unconscious assumptions have *you* made about your life—and death? How do you define "old age"? And how do you think old age should be regarded? What have you passed on to younger people about old age and death? Have you merely handed them your own prejudices and unconscious assumptions? Are you willing to examine yourself honestly and admit that perhaps you've been steered through life by ideas and notions which simply were foolish and which should be discarded because they interfere with your happiness and well-being?

For those of you who may not have had any number at all come to mind as you read the question, don't worry. There's nothing wrong with that. It may be simply that you haven't got any such idea in mind—that you're living your life on a more open-ended basis. In either case, however, the time has come to really look clearly at what your life is all about and how you may be remembered when you're gone.

An obituary is an objective statement of fact. It is both a death notice and a summary of the person's life. You are now going to write your own obituary, stating the facts of your life as they are to date and—using your imagination—as you'd like them to be for the rest of your life or, perhaps, as you're afraid they'll be. Obituaries are usually not very long, so this isn't a major writing assignment. But it is a major assignment in terms of *life assessment*—your values, your relations with other people, your accomplishments, your success as a provider, spouse, parent, friend, and citizen.

That last word may bring to mind the memorable film, *Citizen Kane*, which can be thought of as a cinematic obituary. For all Kane's wealth and power, he died unhappy, unloved, unwanted. His life influenced many but touched none. Through all his vast achievements in political power and social status, through all his financial empire, through all his priceless works of art and real estate, Citizen Kane was searching blindly for the happiness he had known as a child. And as he lay dying, the word "rosebud"—his final utterance—summed up his life. As a little boy, simply playing with his Rosebud sled had been total satisfaction. Yet in growing up, he lost the simplicity of his childhood and began trying to recapture it, ruthlessly, desperately, because his existence—seemingly so awesome and important in the eyes of the world—was to Kane himself empty and unfulfilled. His end was miserable.

Is that how yours will be? I hope not, but only you can say. In any case, now—right now—is a good time to take stock of your life. Have you been a "friend to man"? How will your spouse remember you? Your neighbors? Your work associates? Who will eulogize you, and what will be said, and will it be sincere? If you have children, what character development and values have they learned from you, consciously through your training or non-consciously through imitating your example? If you are in some kind of supervisory position in business, education, or the military, how will those under you regard your passing? In short, who will miss you and what will be the effect of your life on the world?

If death seems fearful because your life will have been meaningless, whose fault is that? Isn't it clear that the meaning of your life is entirely in your control? It grows out of your values, your character, your relations with others, your accomplishments, your sacrifices, and your gifts of love, honesty, tolerance, sympathy, understanding, helpfulness, courage, fairness, loyalty, courtesy, cheerfulness. These are not commodities to be bought and sold. They are yours, entirely within your control. They are the basis of meaning in your life. Without them, human existence is cruel and bleak, no matter how wealthy or famous or powerful you might be. Consider this as you write your own obituary. When you have finished, think deeply upon this:

My death will be reported like this someday. Will my life have been worthwhile?

Obituary

Disregard inapplicable blanks.

_____died today at the age
(Your full name)
of_____. A resident of _____
                                (your home town)
he/she died of _____
_____
_____

(Describe how and where—e.g., sudden illness/long illness at home/hospital, in a highway accident, etc. Be specific.)

He/she is best remembered for_____

_____

_____

_____

_____

(How people will remember you)

He/she was the_____

(Husband/wife/son/daughter)

of _____

(Name)

He/she was born on _____

(Date)

in _____

(Location)

and received his/her education at_____

(School and/or college)

_____. where he/she studied

_____

(Subject/s)

After graduation, he/she joined the _____

_____

(Business/other organization)

and worked there_____years.

He/she is survived by_____

_____

_____

_____

(People in your family who will live longer than you.)

Details of the funeral and _____

(Burial/cremation)

are as follows: _____

_____

_____

(What kind of funeral/disposition of the body do you want?)

_____

I am indebted to teacher-counselor Timothy Ring, M.A., of Waterbury, Connecticut, for the basic format of this obituary. It is an exercise he uses in his death awareness course, and I have expanded it here.

If your obituary leaves you feeling unsatisfied, remorse-
ful, angry, disappointed—anything less than serene and
tranquil—then think deeply upon this: *It is within my
power to change it by changing my life*. Don't mistake a
change in your outward circumstances, however, for the
kind of change I'm talking about here. Perhaps part of your
fear of dying involves guilt over a wrong you committed—
say, an insult or lie. If so, you should correct it and clear
your conscience. This is not only morally right, it is also in
your own best interest because it will relieve you of some
of the death-fear you harbor. As Dr. Bernie Siegel, author of
Love, Medicine and Miracles, says, "Don't wait until you're
going to die to start living."

Changes of this sort—changes in values, character traits,
relations with others, attitudes toward friends, relatives,
fellow workers, even "enemies"—are immediately possible for you. The results can be marvelously freeing, as
you will see demonstrated in the lives of certain people
whom the world regards as saints and heroes. Chapter 11
will present some of them. The next chapter, however, will
offer you further practice in "living your dying."

8
Practice Exercises for Learning to Die

A man who dies before he dies
Does not know when he dies.
Abraham á Sancta Clara

Learning to do anything well requires sustained practice and varied exercises that deepen your skill and understanding. Dying is no exception—dying well, that is. In this chapter, therefore, you will perform some practical exercises that can familiarize you with the idea that someday you will die. Not only will they desensitize you and help break the automatic fear reaction you have whenever confronted with an aspect of death, they will also build your courage to deliberately confront death-fear in *all* life situations, and thus someday die a good death.

"I die daily," said St. Paul in his first epistle to the Corinthians. This simple statement sums up the wisdom offered to you by those who have transcended fear of dying. To die daily is to *practice* your dying until fearlessness becomes as automatic as your previous fear reaction was. As the near-death experience taught those who went through it, death itself is not painful, but rather is comfortable and even blissful. It is only the fearful anticipation of pain, loss, meaninglessness, the unknown, and nonbeing that makes dying appear so awful.

The near-death experiencers learned this in one powerful lesson. However, an actual near-death situation will not be required of you here! But you will *simulate* the death experience, continuing to reinforce what you have already learned in previous chapters. You will cast out fear even more.

In *To Die With Style* Marjorie Caseliser McCoy writes:

> *Perhaps it is by trust that I can achieve my death. To be aware of myself—my feelings, my beliefs, my aspirations—and trust that self. To discover a style that expresses myself in the best way and trust that style. To explore the implications of my style of living for the way I want to achieve my death and trust the changes that may ensue. To be able finally to integrate my view of death and my view of life and live in the reality of both. This, it seems to me, is the central task of living that offers a glorious possibility—to live in trust, to make choices that include my dying, to experience that final creative surge. I can achieve my death. I can live and die—with style.*

There is much talk nowadays about styles of living, but not about styles of dying. However, by deliberating on developing your *deathstyle*, you automatically enhance your *lifestyle*—not in a material sense, of course, but in the richness and joy with which you experience each passing moment, each relationship, each situation and circumstance, day by day.

The exercises that follow come from many sources, and are by no means exhaustive of what has been developed by psychologists and counselors. Some are of my own devising also. Don't try to hurry through them all at once. Rather, choose one and work with it *thoroughly* until you feel familiar with it and are genuinely pleased with your results. One exercise a day is probably all you should attempt, and probably you should spend several days or more on each one. But you be the judge and set whatever pace seems best for you.

Prior to beginning these, obtain a pen and notebook and keep them with you throughout your practice. You will record various experiences, memories, insights, feelings, and intentions in the notebook so that you have a permanent record of your accomplishments and your progress.

1. DEATH PERSONALIZATION. This exercise, similar to the one in Chapter 7, is adapted from an appendix to a research report by Dr. Charles Garfield, which we will examine in detail in Chapter 9. The part his research subjects performed is given in quotes. I have embellished it with further instructions.

In a quiet, moderately-lit room or some other setting where you can write without distraction, sit comfortably with your pen and notebook. At a desk or table would be best. Allow one half-hour in which to be alone. Then read the following instructions and begin to write.

"Someday in the future you will die. Please write a brief but complete and detailed description of this event as you imagine it will actually happen. Imagine and include in your description such concrete details as your age, place, cause of death, physical surroundings, etc. Be specific about your last thoughts and feelings. Use your imagination freely, perhaps picturing the scene in your mind as you imagine it. Finally draw a picture of your burial marker and indicate your epitaph etched in stone."

2. FOLLOW-UP ON DEATH PERSONALIZATION. Sometime after you have completed Exercise 1, begin to consider your reactions as you wrote the description of your death. As you recall your response, record it in your notebook following the description. Was it total anxiety or did you feel something else—mild relief, perhaps, or even a sense of transcendence at being able to view somewhat objectively what had previously seemed so fearful?

3. PRETEND IT IS YOUR LAST HOUR ON EARTH. Allow one hour for this exercise. Take the full sixty minutes to enter into the role of having just one hour left to live. Assume that your legal and financial affairs are in order. You will be concerned here only with the psychological and emotional aspects of this experience.

Use real force of imagination to become a person who has one hour of life left. You may choose to lie down on a couch or bed, as if you were terminally ill. In that case, dim the lights. Loosen any wearing apparel that constricts your breathing or circulation or that is uncomfortable. Remove distracting items such as watches, hair combs, wallets, and pocket change. Use a clock which you can see to mark the hour. Have your pen and notebook handy. Or you may choose to walk around freely, using your senses to experience the life around you. In that case, no special preparation is necessary except to carry your pen and notebook.

Enter into the situation fully. What would you want to do if you had one hour left? Who would you want to see— and why? What would you want to say, if anything? Is there any special experience that seems most appropriate or desirable in those circumstances? If so, what feelings accompany it? Love? Anger? Fear? Remorse? Humor? A desire for revenge? Compassion? Gratitude? Forgiveness?

Record your experiences when the hour is up. Read over them several days later and see how you regard this exercise.

4. IMAGINE YOUR OWN FUNERAL. In a darkened room, sit quietly or lie down. You may use a chair, couch, or even stretch out on the floor. Loosen all constricting or uncomfortable items of wearing apparel; remove distracting items such as watches, hair combs, wallets, and pocket change. Have your pen and notebook handy.

Then close your eyes and visualize yourself laid out in a casket for the wake. You may tape record the following paragraphs and play them to yourself as an aid to visualization. If so, speak the words slowly and allow long pauses in order to fully explore the situation mentally as you listen to the playback. Your hands are crossed in front of you at waist level. You have certain items of dress that have been picked out by your survivors. What are you wearing?

The lid of the casket is open and people are beginning to file past the casket. Who comes to view you laid out? Is there anyone you are surprised to see? As the people come up to your casket, what are they saying? How do they look? Is there anyone you wish had come, but hasn't? Why hasn't he or she come?

Now the people begin to approach your survivors seated nearby in order to offer condolences. How do your survivors look? What emotions do they show? What do they say to each other? Who comes to view you laid out? What are their emotions and expressions? What do they say to your survivors?

Now the scene changes to the funeral service. Your casket remains as before, opened and in the same setting. A minister, priest, or rabbi conducts the funeral service. A eulogy is delivered. Who delivers it? What does he or she say? After the service, your survivors approach the coffin for their final look at you. How do they appear? What are their expressions, their words, their gestures?

Then your survivors are led away to a limousine while funeral home personnel close your casket. Pallbearers place it in a hearse and drive to the gravesite, where they place it over the grave, ready to be lowered. The minister, priest, or rabbi offers some prayers. When graveside ceremonies are completed, the coffin is lowered into the ground. Your survivors drop some earth on top of the casket, and the funeral ends as they walk away. Later, cemetery personnel fill in the grave with the earth piled beside it. You are now interred.

Cease visualizing and remain quiet for several minutes as you experience your own funeral. When you want to, open your eyes, reorient yourself, stretch and get up. Then record your impressions about your interment.

5. CERTIFY YOUR OWN DEATH. By law, a certificate of death must be filled out for everyone upon their expiration. In this exercise, you are going to fill out your own death certificate. The certificate is one used in my home state, Connecticut, but is similar to those used in your own location. Notice that many signatures are required on the certificate—physician, medical examiner, funeral director, embalmer, registrar of vital statistics, and the informant who provided personal information about you. Thus, you will be playing all those roles, in addition to being the deceased.

As you assume each role, try to actually enter the state of

mind you think likely for that person. How does your death seem to each of them? If it seems quite impersonal, are you satisfied with being considered as just another statistic? What seems important about your life that will *not* be recorded on the certificate of death? Now begin to fill out the certificate on pages 72-73.

6. LISTEN TO SPECIAL MUSIC. This exercise was described to me by Dr. Kenneth Ring, who originated it in his counseling work. It requires that you obtain a recording of Richard Strauss' *Death and Transfiguration*. The piece lasts about twenty minutes, and you should allow another twenty minutes for possible personal response to it.

In a dimly lit room, sit quietly or lie down. You may use a chair, couch, or even stretch out on the floor. Loosen all constricting or uncomfortable wearing apparel; remove distracting items such as watches, hair combs, wallets and pocket change. Have your pen and notebook nearby so you can record your thoughts and feelings afterward.

Take a few minutes to relax and quiet your mind. Then turn on your phonograph or tape recording, and resume your position. Simply listen to the music. Let it flow into you. Try to feel it throughout your being. Don't try to analyze your thoughts or feelings—just flow with the music. If emotions arise, don't suppress them. *Express* them—let them out. When the music has finished, lie still and listen to the silence for a while, allowing your consciousness to wander freely. When it feels right, get up and record in your notebook all you can remember— images that came to mind, insights you had, feelings of fear or oblivion, etc., and anything that crossed your mind as something to be accomplished, such as contacting a lawyer about your will or simply contacting a friend to share your feeling of affection for him or her.

7. VIDEOTAPE YOUR FINAL FAREWELL. Because television technology is so widespread, dying people have begun to leave videotaped farewells for their families and friends. This is a uniquely modern way to do what has otherwise

been done through the ages—saying goodbye to people through writing, to offer them comfort and to ensure that, if a person cannot avoid death, at least he can live on in the memories of his loved ones and of coming generations.

Eighteen-year-old Paulette Kizzar, a cystic fibrosis patient from Santa Ana, California, died in a hospital in January 1987, hours after saying tearfully to the camera, "I just want everybody to remember me—not like I look right now, but how I was always smiling and having a good time. And I don't want anybody to ever think that I'm a quitter, because I'm going to fight it as long and as hard as I can. And if I die, I want everybody to be happy for me because I won't have to have treatments. I won't have to go to the doctors anymore."

Hugh B. Montgomery of Bailey, Colorado, died at home at age 57, after a fifteen-year bout with cancer which he told no one about until his condition became obvious. Because he had long been active and public-minded in civic affairs, he was widely mourned. Ten days before his death, he made a videotaped communication summarizing for the world his philosophy of life, arising from his long acquaintance with impending death and its effect on living. As a memorial to him, his wife, Pat, has made copies of the videotape available. I've listed it in Appendix 3. It is a moving experience to see Hugh lying on his deathbed, speaking calmly of life and love and health and healthy relationships.

You, too, can use videotape to reflect upon the quality and meaning of your life and relationships in anticipation of your eventual demise. You might even specify that it be shown at your funeral—a final gesture to your survivors and friends of your love for them. Eulogies are good words spoken at a funeral when it is too late for the person being remembered to hear the words. Videotaping your own "good words" about others can be a eulogy in reverse. (Of course, you should also share your good words with the people they're about *before* you and they die, and it's too late for them to know of your appreciation. Why save eulogies for funerals?)

Set up a loaded videocamera in a room where you can be alone and undisturbed. Aim it at a chair where you will sit or a bed where you will lay. Focus at what you feel is the appropriate distance; a close-up on your face or a medium shot on your upper torso and head is probably best. Then set the camera on automatic, take your place, and, after quieting yourself, project yourself mentally into a situation in which you are very close to death but have sufficient strength and clarity of mind to speak to those who will survive you.

Speak from the heart. Say all you'd want them to know if you actually were dying. Recall warm memories, hopes, dreams. Ask forgiveness for wrongs you committed; offer forgiveness for wrongs done to you. Share your most intimate thoughts, and when you have completed your goodbyes, turn off the camera.

Wait several days before reviewing the tape, in order to let the experience stand on its own. Then watch the tape to evaluate it critically, not so much for its production value as for its emotional quality and its effectiveness in conveying the message you want to give to others. Repeat the exercise as appropriate.

When you feel you have achieved what you want, place the videotape in a safe place, suitably marked with instructions for your survivors. You should tell someone else— your spouse, attorney, or a friend—of its existence. You can even include instructions in your will about use of the videotape in your funeral proceedings.

In addition to these exercises, you should take whatever other opportunities are available to you for becoming accustomed (but not insensitive!) to death and dying. There may, for example, be a funeral director who is sympathetic and willing to show you through his facilities, including the preparation room. It may also be possible for you to visit a crematory or a morgue. If you are near a museum in which there is a mummy, spend some time in a quiet contemplation of the mummy. Walk through a cemetery. Stop quietly beside a grave for awhile. Contemplate the

CERTIFICATE OF DEATH
CONN. STATE DEPT. OF HEALTH

DECEASED—NAME	FIRST	MIDDLE	LAST	SEX		STATE FILE NUMBER
1.				2.		

DATE OF BIRTH (MONTH, DAY, YEAR)	RACE—WHITE, NEGRO, AMERICAN INDIAN, ETC. (SPECIFY)	AGE— LAST BIRTHDAY (YEARS)	UNDER 1 YEAR		UNDER 1 DAY		DATE OF DEATH (MONTH, DAY, YEAR)
			MOS.	DAYS	HOURS	MIN.	
1.	4.	5a.	5b.		5c.		6.

COUNTY OF DEATH	TOWN OF DEATH	HOSPITAL OR OTHER INSTITUTION— NAME (IF NOT IN EITHER, GIVE STREET AND NUMBER)
3.		7c.
7a.	7b.	

CITY & STATE OF BIRTH (Country, if not U.S.)	CITIZEN OF (Country)	MARRIED, NEVER MARRIED, WIDOWED, DIVORCED, LEGALLY SEPARATED	LAST SPOUSE (If wife, give maiden name)
	8b.	9.	10.
8a.			

SOCIAL SECURITY NUMBER	USUAL OCCUPATION (GIVE KIND OF WORK DONE DURING MOST OF WORKING LIFE, EVEN IF RETIRED)	KIND OF BUSINESS OR INDUSTRY
11.	12a.	12b.

RESIDENCE—STATE	COUNTY	TOWN	STREET AND NUMBER
13a.	13b.	13c.	13d.

WAS DECEASED A VETERAN? (SPECIFY YES OR NO)	IF YES, GIVE WAR	UNIT OR SHIP
14a.	14b.	14c.

FATHER—NAME	FIRST	MIDDLE	LAST	MOTHER—MAIDEN NAME	FIRST	MIDDLE	LAST
15.				16.			

INFORMANT—NAME	MAILING ADDRESS (STREET OR R.F.D. NO., CITY OR TOWN, STATE, ZIP)
17a.	17b.

PART I. DEATH WAS CAUSED BY: (ENTER ONLY ONE CAUSE PER LINE FOR (a), (b), AND (c)

		APPROXIMATE INTERVAL BETWEEN ONSET AND DEATH
18.	IMMEDIATE CAUSE	
CONDITIONS, IF ANY WHICH GAVE RISE TO IMMEDIATE CAUSE (a), STATING THE UNDERLYING CAUSE LAST	(a)	
	DUE TO, OR AS A CONSEQUENCE OF:	
	(b)	
	DUE TO, OR AS A CONSEQUENCE OF:	
	(c)	

PART II. OTHER SIGNIFICANT CONDITIONS: CONDITIONS CONTRIBUTING TO DEATH BUT NOT RELATED TO CAUSE GIVEN IN PART I (a)

	AUTOPSY (YES OR NO) 19a.	IF YES WERE FINDINGS CONSIDERED IN DETERMINING CAUSE OF DEATH 19b.

| | (ENTER NATURE OF INJURY PART I OR PART II, ITEM 18) 19i. | INJURY AT WORK (SPECIFY YES OR NO) 20e. |

ACCIDENT, SUICIDE, HOMICIDE OR UNDETERMINED (SPECIFY)
20a.

DATE OF INJURY (MONTH, DAY, YEAR)
20b.

HOUR
20c. M.

HOW INJURY OCCURRED
20d.

PLACE OF INJURY AT HOME, FARM, STREET, FACTORY, OFFICE BLDG., ETC. (SPECIFY)
20f.

LOCATION (STREET OR R.F.D. NO., CITY OR TOWN, STATE)
20g.

SURGERY RELEVANT TO CONDITION REPORTED IN ITEM 18 *(Date performed)* (Name of operation)
20h.   20i.

CERTIFICATION—PHYSICIAN: I ATTENDED THE DECEASED FROM
21a.

MONTH DAY YEAR
TO
21b.

MONTH DAY YEAR
21c.

AND LAST SAW HIM/HER ALIVE ON
MONTH DAY YEAR
21d.

DEATH OCCURRED ON THE DATE, AND, TO THE BEST OF MY KNOWLEDGE, DUE TO THE CAUSE(S) STATED.
(HOUR)   M.

CERTIFICATION—MEDICAL EXAMINER: IN MY OPINION, ON THE DATE AND HOUR OF DEATH DUE TO THE CAUSE(S) STATED, DEATH RESULTED ON OR ABOUT
22a.   M.

THE DECEDENT WAS PRONOUNCED DEAD
MONTH   DAY   YEAR   HOUR
22b.   M.

CERTIFIER—NAME (TYPE OR PRINT)
23a.

SIGNATURE
23b.

DEGREE OR TITLE

DATE SIGNED (MONTH, DAY, YEAR)
23d.

MAILING ADDRESS—CERTIFIER
23c.

STREET OR R.F.D. NO.   CITY OR TOWN   STATE   ZIP   CITY OR TOWN   STATE

BURIAL, CREMATION, REMOVAL (SPECIFY)
24a.

CEMETERY OR CREMATORY—NAME
24b.

LOCATION
24c.

DATE (MONTH, DAY, YEAR)
24d.

FUNERAL HOME—NAME AND ADDRESS (STREET OR R.F.D. NO., CITY OR TOWN, STATE, ZIP)
25a.

FUNERAL DIRECTOR OR EMBALMER—SIGNATURE
26a.

NAME OF EMBALMER
26a.

IF BODY WAS EMBALMED

LICENSE NUMBER
26b.

THIS CERTIFICATE RECEIVED FOR RECORD ON
27a.

BY
27b.

REGISTRAR

life of the one who is buried there, and then let your awareness expand to encompass the lives of all the other people buried in the cemetery. Finally, meditate in your own fashion—perhaps using an exercise from chapter 9—being mindful that you, too, will someday share the condition of those around you.

As I've said before, if you can't change your fate, change your attitude. Rock singer Rod Stewart offers a good example of following this advice, showing courage and creativity in facing death. A decade ago he told reporters that he was once obsessed with dying before he tackled his fears directly. "I had a phobia about it," Stewart said. "Some people have it about flying. Well, I had it about dying. God know why! I just suddenly understood that we all had to die. I thought the only way I was going to overcome this was to face it—so I took a job in Highgate Cemetery digging graves."

Death may be inevitable, but that's no reason to fear it!

9
Meditation—The World's Best Fear Remover

We have already hit upon a few hints toward developing exercises for a Craft of Dying. For example . . . we could practice being alone, and practice feeling at home in the presence of the unknown.

I can imagine a very simple practice which would fulfill these requirements. In order to be alone I could practice withdrawing my attention from all objects and persons that occupy the space that surrounds me and direct it exclusively toward internal states. I could rehearse this gesture of rupture with my "world," the prop that supports my "reality," by reversing the flow of my attention from the tendency toward dispersal in space to a concentration in time. Skill in performing this gesture would require practice, and would constitute a technique for simulating the radical solitude of the encounter with death. But we must also learn how to be at home in the presence of the unknown. What is called for is another gesture of consciousness, this time directed toward dropping the efforts to make everything knowable. The mind, instead of striving continually to grasp things, must be coaxed into letting go. The work of trying to force things into conceptual schemes would have to give way to the play of simply being aware. If knowing is an activity, being aware is a non-activity or non-doing; if awareness is a challenge and a conquest, unknowing of awareness is a surrender and a relinquishment. This practice of dying has another, more familiar name: It is called "meditation."

Michael Grosso, "The Mirror of
Transformation," *Theta*, 1977

Death has been of central consideration in all the world's major religious and spiritual paths, and each has worked out a variety of ways with which to eliminate fear of dying. Meditation is the principal method they use. It has been called "the craft of dying." Therefore when I said in the Preface that no one had systematically described how to deal with fear of your own death, I was referring to popular literature. I could have qualified my statement (but for literary reasons it seemed inappropriate at that point) by saying "with the exception of the great spiritual traditions."

This chapter will introduce you to meditation in a highly simplified and limited way. It will also give you some meditation exercises to help you allay your fear of death and dying. Since meditation is widely discussed nowadays, you're probably familiar with it in at least a small way. Many books on it are available. One of mine, an anthology entitled *What Is Meditation?* (Anchor Press, 1974) offers an overview of the various meditative traditions and practices. In my Introduction, I made the following point.

Meditation is a means of personal and transpersonal growth. It is a time-honored technique—probably humanity's oldest spiritual discipline—for helping people release their potential for expanded consciousness and fuller living. Also a technique for assisting in the enlightenment process of directly knowing God or ultimate reality, meditation appears in some form in nearly every major religious tradition. The entranced yogi in a lotus posture, the Zen Buddhist sitting in zazen, the Christian contemplative kneeling in adoration of Jesus, the Sufi dervish whirling in an ecstasy-inducing state—all can be properly described as practicing meditation. Although the cultural or religious trappings may vary, meditation's core experience is an altered state of consciousness in which your ordinary sense of "I"—the ego—is diminished, while a larger sense of self-existence-merged-with-the-cosmos comes into awareness.

When your self-centered consciousness is dissolved, your true identity shines through. This is enlightenment, cosmic consciousness, union with God. The experience is transforming. Your life changes because you realize the essential truth of what spiritual teachers, sages, and saints have said: Death as nonexistence is an illusion, there is nothing to fear, and it is only your petty little ego that generates the fear, along with the sorrow, greed, jealousy, pride, lust, and all the other sins, vices, and unfulfilling desires that make life miserable for you and for others.

Later in this chapter, you'll have some actual experience with meditation. First, however, I think it will be most worthwhile to hear about a unique scientific study that investigated the relationship between meditation and reduced fear of death. It was conducted in 1973-74 by Dr. Charles Garfield, a clinical research psychologist at the University of California, Berkeley, and its associated Cancer Research Institute across the bay in San Francisco. (You'll hear more about Garfield in Chapter 14.) He reported the findings in his book, *Rediscovery of the Body* (Dell, 1977). I will summarize and quote from his chapter, "Ego Functioning, Fear of Death, and Altered States of Consciousness."

Garfield analyzed the conscious and unconscious fear of death in members of five distinct groups: Graduate students in psychology, graduate students in religion, psychedelic-drug users (specifically, those who systematically used LSD-25), Zen meditators, and American-born disciples of Tibetan Buddhism. His purpose was to measure the similarities and differences within and between the groups' reactions to death in order to determine if there was a correlation between the systematic alteration of consciousness and the intensity of a person's fear of death.

First, he took extensive clinical interviews with his subjects. Then he assessed their physiological responses by measuring their galvanic skin response (which is what a lie detector does) and their heart rate fluctuation following exposure to death-related items on a word-association task. Last of all, he measured the same physiological functions during an exercise in which each subject wrote a description of his own death. (This is the exercise I included in Chapter 8.)

What Garfield found was this: Whereas the psychology and religion students showed significant differences between their measurements before and during the word association exercise, the Zen meditators and Tibetan Buddhists did not. The drug users were somewhere between. Likewise, in the death personalization exercise, the psychology and religion students showed much greater "phobic sensitivity" to the death-related stimuli.

In discussing his research, Garfield wrote:

> The results of this investigation appear to support the assertion that individuals who have long-term systematic experiences with altered-state disciplines such as meditation or the psychedelics are less afraid of death than individuals without such experience. . . . The graduate students . . . responded with greater emotional intensity . . . to death-related words than to words selected from a general language sample. The subjects in the "altered-state" groups . . . did not manifest significant differences in their responses to the two word groups. Similarly, the students' physiological responses . . . during the death personalization exercise were consistently greater than those of the altered-state subjects during the same exercise. These results are especially significant if we consider the fear associated with this exercise to be a more specifically personal death-fear than that connected with the word-association task, which confronts subjects with some of the non-personal aspects of death. These findings indicate that altered state groups may exhibit less fear not only of personal extinction (i.e., "ceasing to be") but also of such seemingly related factors as pain, loss of cognitive/affective control, loss of "significant others" (i.e., family, friends, loved ones).

How does consciousness-alteration through meditation°
help to reduce fear of death and dying? In an earlier report

°I am deliberately disregarding consideration of the psychedelic drug users in this discussion for a variety of reasons. First, the data on them are less significant than the data on the meditators. In other words, meditation is more effective than dope. Second, psychedelics are illegal. In addition, psychedelics are not always available, and their quality and dosage varies, whereas meditation on the investigation, "Consciousness Alteration and Fear of Death," which Garfield published in 1975 in the *Journal of Transpersonal Psychology*, he noted that the habitually-preferred mode of consciousness for Western civilization is one which stresses hyperrationality, willful control of faculties, emotions and situations, and outward-directed awareness toward others (but more as objects to be manipulated than as people with whom to openly relate).

This is a sort of operational definition of the ego, which places itself in center-stage of everything and attempts to make everything and everyone subservient to its incessant demands for being number one. Anything that tends to reduce the ego, Garfield says, is perceived as threatening and is likely to induce anxiety.

> If the fear of death is fundamentally the fear of egoic extinction, or ceasing to be, then perhaps this fear can be influenced by those ego-loss experiences described as basic to various altered states of consciousness. This suggests the possibility that individuals with considerable altered-state experience may have somehow found a means to temporarily experience their own non-being. If this is the case, they might be expected to exhibit a diminished fear of death.

To return to Garfield's principal research report, he notes that Western civilization rarely presents any self-acceptable loss-of-control experiences. Thus, when a Westerner confronts the reality of his own death—the seemingly irreversible loss of control and rationality—he

---

is available to you in endless supply and you always know what you're getting. Since the emphasis in this book is on the *practical*, I won't examine psychedelic drugs as a means of dealing with death-fear, except for a footnote in Chapter 15.

However, you should be aware that there is competent research indicating that LSD-25 can be very useful in doing just that, although legislation has now shut off further studies. The best account of the subject is *The Human Encounter with Death* by Drs. Stanislav Grof and Joan Halifax. They report dramatic results through psychedelic therapy in reducing fear of dying among patients at the Spring Grove, Maryland hospital.

has no past resources by which to gauge or deal with this internal experience. The individual feels both dependent and inadequate. In a sense, Garfield says, the ego is no longer master of its own fate or the captain of the self. Then he makes this important point:

> It cannot be overemphasized that these fears of dependency, regression, and loss of self-control are culturally induced. Ego dissolution . . . which for the Westerners may constitute the core of death-fear, appears to be precisely the state of consciousness so adamantly pursued by the esoteric core of Eastern religion. In fact, Freud's description of the operation of Thanatos, the death instinct, approximates, if not duplicates, phenomenological accounts of the Eastern notion of the highest state of consciousness, i.e., satori, nirvana, etc.

That last sentence touches on the reason I said in Chapter 1 that there was an ironic twist in what Freud said about death. What he saw as the end is really, from the perspective of higher consciousness, just the beginning—a transition, not a termination. Freud observed in people the potential to transcend the ego, but because of his own limitations, he failed to understand the true significance of what he observed. He gave it a negative interpretation. Remember what Freud said: In the unconscious, every one of us is convinced of our immortality. Spiritual traditions reply to Freud: We are unconsciously convinced because, in truth, we really *are* deathless. The true self cannot die, being one with God, Brahman, the Tao, the all-creative Void. The true self is universal, cosmically conscious. There are no limits to it except the illusory one we create, called ego—the false idea, which we nevertheless believe, that a separate, independent self is the essential "me" and "you." *That* self—the ego—is indeed mortal because it has identified with a perishable body. To think that the ego is immortal is, as Freud saw, the basis of mental illness and suffering. He, therefore, gave a negative interpretation to our intuition of immortality. Because he did not see beyond the ego, he failed to distinguish the false from the true, and extolled the virtues of being tightly in control, as he himself was, even to the point of stoically bearing the pain of throat cancer from which he eventually died.*

But as Zen exponent Alan Watts points out, most notably in his *Psychotherapy East and West*, meditation does not result in mere loss of ego functioning. Rather, it culminates in a mode of awareness in which the duality of ego and world, the split between self and not-self, "I" and environment, is seen through as an illusion, and the essential unity of all things is directly experienced. A sense of self remains, but that self has a new identity, a cosmic identity. Claire Myers Owens, who began Zen training at the age of 74, describes it this way in her absorbing memoirs, *Zen and the Lady*. One day, after six arduous years of Zen discipline,

> I slipped out of bed and placed the bed pillows on the floor to begin a meditation unlike any other I had known.....My body immediately settled itself into a comfortable and proper posture. I sat with a "sense of dignity and grandeur—like a mountain."
>
> I sat on and on—an hour? two hours? in full lotus position—motionless. Gradually my hands melted into each other. My knees were pierced by pain. My back was aching. All this was occurring at some far distance. Trivial matters like pain did not concern me.
>
> As time passed my body grew heavier than heavy, like some great rock embedded in the earth, like some great tree strongly rooted in the deep immovable—indestructible.
>
> I wanted never again to move my body, never again to change anything. Any state into which I might move, a state of power—wealth—fame—love—passion—could not compare with the serene state of being I was in at this moment. It was peace—deep unutterable peace.
>
> I seemed to have arrived at the end of a long journey, the end of a rough road that had offered many inspiring

---

*Incidentally, insofar as disease is "body language," it is interesting to speculate that Freud's throat cancer was a psychosomatic expression of unvoiced doubts about his psychoanalytic doctrines and unvoiced guilt over not honestly admitting that there might be something positive and real to those promptings of immortality after all.

views along the way. It was a beautiful plateau on which I might rest indefinitely, at which I had arrived after years of striving on the path.

I felt no desire, no ambition, no regrets. No words can describe such perfection, such completeness, fulfillment and finality.

I was intensely aware of my body yet I felt suspended bodiless in a new height. Everything within me seemed to vibrate gently in a golden light. Then everything within me was in utter stillness—like an eternal stillness. Nothing anywhere except ineffable quietness and inexpressible stillness.

I did not feel the self fuse with the absolute. I felt that the whole universe—everything that is—the uncreated—changeless, beginningless—everlasting—was in me—*was* me—for a fleeting forever.

Everything was intangible, invisible, formless, and colorless—beyond the reach of the senses, above the grasp of conceptual thinking, beyond words—yet real as only reality can be. Everything was nothingness. Nothingness was everythingness.

Was it the end of everything or the beginning for me? Was it a glimpse of the bliss of life after death? All fear of death vanished right away—forever.

I will conclude this summary of Garfield's report with a long quote that capsulizes the data he obtained from the clinical interviews he conducted with his research subjects.

If we are willing to venture into new territories to better understand the process of dying, we may have to control our aversion to relinquishing rational self-control and our anxiety around the blurring or loss of ego-boundaries. An analysis of the clinical data I obtained through extensive clinical interviews with individuals who had long-term systematic experience in consciousness alteration and controls revealed that altered-state subjects consistently manifested less fear of the following phenomena: (1) ego dissolution, cessation of thought, and the permanence of egoic annihilation in physical death; (2) loss of control and fluctuation in the level of cognitive and affective control; (3) ambiguity, logical paradox, and paralogical process; taxing one's psychologic resources beyond the limits of

traditional methods of logico-deductive problem solving;
(4) the unknown and the irreversibility of death; (5) loss of
bodily functioning; distortions in body image equated not
only with loss of function but decreased self-esteem as well;
(6) regression; a shift from the world of social/material
reality to a primary world of oceanic experience; (7) loss of
significant others, i.e., family, friends, etc.; (8) dependency
and/or passivity; mental/physical decline which they do
not equate with personal inadequacy; (9) the dying process
and the association among dying, pain, and physical
deterioration. Fear of many of these factors is deeply en-
grained and not easily modifiable. However, one may
hypothesize—as many of the interviewed altered-state
subjects did—that repeated experiences with ego-death
contribute to a patient's ability to accept (feel comfortable
with) a temporary loss of rational control.

Are you willing to "venture into new territories" in order
to rid yourself of your fear of dying? Meditation is a powerful means of exploring mind and spirit—the most powerful,
in fact. So much of what people think, feel and do is merely
an automatic, conditioned response, including death-fear.
The aim of meditation is *clarity of consciousness*. It helps
you to be aware of reality *fully* so that your thoughts, feelings, and behavior are free and appropriate, not pro-
grammed by anxiety, desire, hatred, prejudice, social
conventions and so forth. It does this by *de*automatizing
and *de*conditioning you.

How does meditation do this? It creates a sort of mental
distance between you and your mind's activity in which
you can observe it with detachment. Meditation also extends your awareness so that you can actually begin to see
thoughts and feelings come into existence. It shows you
deeper aspects of mind than you are ordinarily aware of.
Thus, the experience of meditation allows you to *dis*identify
with your thoughts and feelings. You *have* them, but you
are *not* them, just as you have a car but are not your car.
The car is merely an instrument you use for certain
purposes; it's not actually you. Likewise, you have thoughts
and feelings, but through meditation you begin to see that
those thoughts and feelings are not the essence of you.

Moreover, they may be inappropriate, immature, un-realistic, automatic responses you were conditioned into as you grew up. In perceiving them this way, their compulsive quality is broken and eventually dissolved through insight into the very process by which they arise in the first place.

We'll begin meditating with a very short, simple exercise. It was first suggested by Stanley Keleman in his book, *Living Your Dying*. He calls it the "Five-Breath Medita-tion." That's all the time it takes—five breaths. But people using it for the first time often report strong emotional experiences and insights. One death education counselor, Dr. Rick Ingrasci, described his use of it in groups, saying, "A lot of feelings come up and some people can't handle them the first time." In your case, however, since you are going to do this meditation exercise in private, you have no need to be conscious of what others may think. Nor do you have to fear that you'll be overwhelmed since you've already been through some strongly emotional experiences in the previous chapters, and have arrived safely here.

The Five-Breath Meditation involves taking successively shorter breaths, as if the fifth one were your last and you die at that moment. The first breath is of normal duration. The second breath should be shortened to about half of the first. The third breath is even shorter—about half as long as the second. The fourth is only half that of the third. Thus, each breath is shorter in time and reduced in oxygen. As you breathe, you should mentally set the context of the experience—a context that says, "I'm dying and about to take my final breath." On the fifth breath, breathe out and hold it. Keep air out of your lungs until you feel un-comfortable. Then begin normal respiration.

While holding the fifth breath and imagining it your last, mentally observe what thoughts and feelings come to mind. Many people have surprising emotional surges. That is unguided fantasy, however, not meditation. The medita-tion consists in *observing* those emotions and thoughts. You watch yourself die but don't become entangled in the drama, keeping your consciousness clear even while powerful feelings and perhaps horrifying images pop up.

When it's over, you will have seen more deeply into your own mind and its operations. If you don't like what you see, you are then free to begin transforming it.

The following meditation exercise can be quite helpful to the transformation. It's one I've devised, based on the suggestion of a friend. I've adopted it from Transcendental Meditation, which is a form of yogic meditation and uses a mantra or special sound that is mentally repeated over and over. The TM mantras are Sanskrit words, but you will use an English word: *Thine*. You should think of it as the condensed meaning of the line from the Lord's Prayer, "Thy will be done." In other words, you will be repeating to yourself a meaningful sound which essentially says, "Thy will be done, O God—not mine." The point of this mantra is to consciously begin "letting go and letting God," reducing the selfish tendency we all have to assert our little ego into the center ring and try to run the whole show. Death, of course, is the ultimate threat to ego, and insofar as we identify ourselves with the ego, we fear death, we try to deny it through self-glorifying activities, we try to avoid it through elaborate "security" measures.

None of that works, though. The only sane alternative is to confront it. In doing so, we find paradoxically that as we become less and less self-centered, more and more cosmically-centered, death becomes less and less frightful. As the constricted consciousness of ego opens up, death is seen to be threatening only to the illusion which we mistook to be our real self. The fear often felt by people when deep in meditation is the ego's response to the perception that it is being "swallowed by infinity." Which is precisely the case! But from the point of self-transcendence, that is exactly what needs to be done. Fear of death is the ego's "recoil from infinity." We'll look at this with greater detail in Chapter 18.

Meditation, as I've said, eliminates the obstacles of mind that prevent clarity of consciousness and full perception of reality. Mindfulness, not mindlessness, is the mark of proper meditation. You expand awareness, not eliminate it. You extinguish egotism, revealing your true self which is one with God and is therefore deathless.

Before giving you instructions, I must make two brief comments about when it's best *not* to meditate. First, do not meditate after a meal because most likely you'll only fall asleep. Your body has mobilized itself to digest food, which reduces blood flow to the brain. Less oxygen is passing through and consequently you get that sleepy feeling. Wait an hour or so to avoid dozing off. Second, don't try to meditate just before going to sleep. You may stay up half the night because meditation can leave you feeling wide awake and charged with energy.

To do this meditation, sit down on a chair or couch. Sit up straight but not rigid. As you meditate, you may find that you relax so much that you slump over to one side, or your head may nod down to your chest. That's okay, but if you become aware of this happening while you meditate, you should gently bring yourself back to the upright position.

Your hands can be folded or resting in your lap—whatever feels comfortable to you. Loosen all wearing apparel that feels tight or binding so that blood circulation and breathing are unrestricted. Remove distracting items such as wallets and pocket change. Breathe through your nose unless there is compelling reason not to. Keep your feet flat on the floor, although if your legs relax and fall to the side, that's also okay. Again, when you become aware of it, gently bring them back to an upright but comfortable position.

Choose a place indoors where the light is not too bright and the noise level is low. Take the telephone off the hook and make sure you're not going to be disturbed for half an hour. Later on, with experience, you may choose to meditate outside.

You're going to meditate for fifteen to twenty minutes. Since meditation tends to take you away from a time-keeping frame of mind, you should have a watch or clock arranged in such a way that you can easily see it without having to change your position. Then you can open your eyes slightly to see how long it's been. Don't be surprised if you think its only been three or four minutes and then open your eyes to find that it's been fifteen. Meditation works that way. (With just a little practice, you'll develop a pretty good sense of when to end your meditation, and the watch or clock won't be necessary any longer.)

To begin, settle yourself comfortably into the meditating position that suits you. Sit quietly with your eyes open for a few moments, without trying to think, and then close your eyes. For perhaps a minute just sit quietly without attempting to say the mantra. Most people normally breathe at a rate of about sixteen breaths per minute, so use your breathing as a guide to time yourself. Just sit there and count sixteen breaths while you let your mind and nervous system settle down. Then silently say to yourself, "Thine." You can say it at whatever speed you want, and you will probably find that you experiment a bit. Try coordinating it with your breathing, and say "Thine" as you breathe out. Just keep saying "Thine" silently in your mind over and over. If your attention wanders away from saying your mantra—which it's almost certain to do—that's all right. That's part of the meditation process. But as soon as you become aware that you have stopped saying your mantra you should gently and effortlessly come back to it. Start repeating, "Thine, Thine, Thine."

During the time your attention is off the mantra, all sorts of interesting thoughts, feelings, and images may come into your field of awareness. That's all right, too. Don't try to stop them forcefully. Carefully but casually observe them, without becoming entangled in them or attached to them. You may start watching an adventuresome drama starring yourself, or recalling various real-life experiences, or pondering some problematic situation. Often the imagery of your meditation will be very insightful, and you'll recall it afterward. Whatever it may be, however, when you become aware that you're not saying the mantra, gently let those thoughts go and begin to repeat the mantra again.

When you've decided to end your meditation, simply stop saying the mantra and sit quietly for about two minutes with your eyes closed. Let your physical senses gradually restore themselves. Then slowly begin to open your eyes. Take the full two minutes to do so, counting breaths if necessary to time it. This serves the purpose of avoiding shock to your nervous system, which is now in a very quiet and sensitized condition.

After the two minutes of "rising to the surface," your eyes will be fully open and you'll be completely aware of your environment. You may have moved your body, hands, or legs somewhat during meditation—it's perfectly okay to do so in this exercise—but you will probably now find yourself in a position that you've been holding in a relaxed way for five or ten minutes, perhaps longer.

Stretch your arms, rub your face and eyes, and get yourself into motion. You'll feel like you're waking up after a good night's sleep, and maybe you'll yawn or heave a deep sigh. But within a few minutes you'll probably feel wide awake and full of energy.

If you wish to modify this meditation with a mantra of your own choosing, feel free to do so. You might prefer to say, "Death will take place," or perhaps, "Death, death, death...." as your mantra. (This is, in fact, an actual Buddhist mindfulness practice. We will examine others in Chapter 10.) And if you wish to explore meditation more—which I heartily recommend—there are many useful books and meditation schools around. A readily-available paperback is *Journey of Awakening* by Daniel Goleman. I also recommend his *The Meditative Mind*. My own *What Is Meditation?* may also be helpful.

When the student is ready, the teacher will appear—in some form, be it a person, a book or an experience. The important thing is to seek. For in the stillness of meditation there can be direct insight into the nature of yourself —an insight that carries conviction beyond all intellectual argument and emotional unburdening. The eternal and immortal creation, from which we are inseparable in its fullness, is our true identity. We are all creation, and forever. Only the ego fears death. But the ego is a false image of ourself, based on attachment to a perishable body. We wrongly and unconsciously identify with this image, and thus *cause ourselves* to suffer. Meditation is the time-honored means for seeing through the illusion that generates suffering and the fear of death.

10
Meditating on Death— The Eastern Craft of Dying

There is much more to be said about meditation as a means of removing death-fear. Volumes could be—and have been—written on it, so I'll make this chapter brief and informational rather than instructional. I simply want to describe to you a bit more about two great Eastern spiritual traditions, Buddhism and Hinduism, and how they develop a tranquil mindfulness of death.

In Tibetan Buddhist monasteries, special ceremonial cups can be seen which are made from the upper portion of the skull of a deceased monk. There are also trumpets made from human thighbones which were likewise taken from the skeleton of a brother monk who died. Over doorways there may be other human bones. These skeletal remains are, from the Buddhist perspective, neither ghoulish nor foolish. They are part of a tradition which aims at cultivating awareness of death in such a way that the monks are eventually serene about the idea of their own death. The skull cups, thighbone trumpets and doorway ornaments are well-meant reminders that reinforce in the monks' consciousness a familiarity and acceptance of mortality.

The principal means by which the monks gain that familiarity and acceptance is meditation—specifically, death meditation. The tradition originated with Buddha, who taught that the only permanent state is nirvana. All else is transitory, though it may take eons to pass away. Death is the chief sign of the impermanence of life. Similarly, life is the chief sign of the impermanence of death. The continuous cycle of death and rebirth can be halted through illuminating insight gained in meditation. When the illusion of ego, the root of selfish desire, has been removed, you enter nirvana. Transcending both life and death, you gain the permanent, the real. We will examine this notion more closely in Chapter 18.

Death meditation has two main forms in the Buddhist tradition. One involves contemplation of the inevitability of death. Thus, the meditator may be instructed to imagine himself as facing an executioner or to reflect on the death of others and then infer his own mortality. Or he may become mindful that no achievement is immune from the possibility of decline and reversal, including all that he hopes for personally. Further contemplation may be made on the unpredictability of death due to illness, accident, murder, war, attack by wild animals, etc. The second form of death meditation may sound even more unpleasant to you, but it has already been mentioned: meditations on corpses. This is used much less than the first form but, nevertheless, it is a tradition within Buddhism for people —primarily monks—to seat themselves near corpses in various states of decay and begin to reflect upon the nature of embodiment.

Ten "foul states" of corpses are described in the ancient Buddhist text, *Vissuddhimagga*. These include meditating on the distorted form of a swollen corpse, meditating on a discolored corpse, meditating on a festering corpse with its horrible stench, meditating on a corpse cut in two, meditating on a cut and dismembered corpse or a bloody one, a worm-eaten one, a badly mangled one, and, last of all, meditating on a skeleton. The psychological benefits of each meditation are also described, such as being a corrective for lust, vanity, the idea that you own your body, etc.

The intended result of these death meditations has been described by Dr. J. Bruce Long in his chapter, "The

Death that Ends Death in Hinduism and Buddhism," which Elisabeth Kübler-Ross included in her book—*Death, The Final Stage of Growth*. Long tells us:

> When the monk realizes within the deepest part of his being that his own life and that of the entire universe is constituted and supported by a compound of birth and death in each and every moment, and when he comes to know that in the end everything returns to ashes, he will obtain a perfect freedom . . . from the illusion that he and the objects of his pleasure are enduing entities. From this insight emerges a cessation of desire to wield the world according to one's own volition. And, with the passing of this habit of living a life of willfullness (and its offspring anxiety and fear) will come automatically a peace of mind and tranquility which will abide unaltered in all conditions of life and all states of mind.

This wisdom has been distilled in a centuries-old Tibetan text intended for lay people as well as monks, the *Bardo Thodol* (or *Bardo Thotrol*), commonly known as *The Tibetan Book of the Dead*. And although the book is obstensibly written for the dead, knowledgeable commentators such as the Tibetan Buddhist teacher, Choygam Trungpa, recently-deceased head of the Naropa Institute in Boulder, Colorado, tell us that the book is in fact about life and for the living.

First translated into English in the 1920s, *The Tibetan Book of the Dead*'s fundamental teaching, Trungpa comments in his version, is "the recognition of one's projections and the dissolutions of the sense of self in the light of reality." Insofar as the book is for use with the dying, the instructions are to be read to them in order to help them maintain the calm, clear meditative state of awareness they cultivated throughout life, and thus to merge with the universe (*samadhi*), becoming one with the luminosity of the void of space from which all existence springs. Ideally, however, *The Tibetan Book of the Dead* is a manual to be studied and memorized throughout life as a means of attaining enlightenment while embodied. Such a person would, at death, recite it to himself and literally dissolve his personal consciousness into the Clear Light of the Void, never again to be born or to die.°

In Hinduism, also, the state of mind of the dying person is considered to be of utmost importance to his ultimate destiny. Thus emphasis is placed on cultivating throughout life a state of mind which will be stabilized in the Real, the True Self which is not subject to the death of the body or other changes in the physical world.

I have already mentioned various yogic practices which pervade Hindu culture. Another is the meditative practice called *pratyahara*, a systematic exercise in sense-withdrawal. The meditator "tunes out" his five senses, one by one, until there is only an internal focus of awareness in which he "rehearses for death." Yogis adept in this practice have been shown under scientific conditions to be totally insensitive to powerful external stimuli. While in the sensory-withdrawal mode, they have been hooked up to EEG machines, which measure brainwaves, and when a loud click is sounded, there has been no interruption in the brainwave pattern. This is quite unlike the normal condition, where a noise, even a soft one, can disturb attention and thereby dramatically alter brainwave patterns. In another experiment, a yogi was touched with a hot test tube that had just been held in a flame. Again, no alteration in brainwaves was noted.

The *Bhagavad Gita*, which is a holy scripture for Hindus, contains instruction on how to die. These instructions, like *The Tibetan Book of the Dead*, encourage the listener to cultivate a state of mind absorbed in ultimate reality, which Hindus call *Brahman*. An article in the July 1976 *Yoga Journal* entitled "How to Die According to the *Bhagavad Gita*," by Dr. John Goyeche, quotes appropriate passages.

°A westernized guidebook inspired by *The Tibetan Book of the Dead* was recently published to bring the teaching into contemporary language and culture. *The American Book of the Dead* by E.J. Gold is available in bookstores and from its publisher, IDHHB, Inc., P. O. Box 370, Nevada City, CA 95959.

Whatever being a man thinks of at the last moment when he leaves his body, that alone does he attain, being ever absorbed in the thought thereof.

The verse immediately preceding this declares:

And whoever, at the time of death, leaving the body, goes forth remembering Me alone, he attains My being, there is no doubt about this.

These verses come from Chapter 8 of the *Bhagavad Gita*. Others on this theme of ours are:

The Omniscient, the Ancient, the Ruler. Minuter than an atom, the Supporter of all, of form inconceivable, effulgent like the sun, and beyond all darkness, he who meditates on this ... at the time of death, with a steady mind, devotion, and strength of yoga, well fixing the entire *prana* (*life energy*) in the middle of the eyebrows, he reaches Him. (8:8)

All the gates of the body closed, the mind confined within the heart, having fixed his life energy in head, engaged in firm yoga, uttering the one-syllabled *OM*, Brahman, thinking of Me, he who departs, leaving the body, attains the Supreme Goal. (8:12-13)

I am easily attainable by that ever-steadfast yogi who constantly remembers Me daily and thinks of nothing else. (8:14)

By thus closing "the doors of the senses" through yogic meditation, the mediator/dying person fixes his consciousness upon the Universal Self, his true identity, and thus enters into a state of spiritual and physical liberation (*mokska*). Like *The Tibetan Book of the Dead*, the *Bhagavad Gita* declares that the frame of mind in which you put yourself at the moment of death will determine the state into which you enter at death. The proper frame of mind is not attained magically, however. Rather, it is cultivated during your life through meditation and pious behavior.

Interestingly, this same view of death and dying is to be found in the medieval Christian volume *Ars Moriendi* or *The Craft of Dying*. It, too, urged that spiritual practices be made a part of the daily life of all who sought to be "at peace with their Maker" or in union with God. Thus it advised:

> When any of likelihood shall die, then it is most necessary
> to have a special friend, the which will heartily help and
> pray for him and therewith counsel the sick for the weal of
> his soul; and moreover to see that all others do so about
> him or else quickly for to make them depart.

In other words, live consciously and die consciously. Do
not fear death; do not hide from it or disguise it from others.
Follow the example of the prophet Isaiah, *The Craft of
Dying* says:

> For when the King Ezechiel lay sick and upon the point
> of death, he (Isaiah) glosed him not, nor used no dissimu-
> lation unto him, but plainly and wholesomely aghasted
> him, saying that he should die.

Meditation in its highest form is not simply an exercise
of mind which one performs in a disciplined way for a
certain period of time each day. Rather, it is *continuous
mindful action* in the midst of daily life. Learning and living
become integrated in spontaneous practice that is actually
no different from whatever you do daily, except for the
state of mind with which you perform it. This is meditation
in action. The meditator has so completely mastered the
lessons of meditation that his entire life is a demonstration
of higher consciousness which can be experienced if
sincerely sought.

For such a person the alteration of consciousness called
meditation has led to a transformation of consciousness—
a permanent state. Meditation in such cases is no longer
just a tool or device. Rather, it is *the person himself*, living
for others as a source of instruction and an example of how
to transcend the fear, suffering, confusion, and selfishness
of the world. People such as this have been recognized
through the ages as special persons for whom attention
and reverence is proper. Now I'd like you to meet some
of them and observe their manner of dying.

11
Dying the Good Death— The Final Hours of Saints and Heroes

In 1963 an extraordinary East Indian spiritual teacher named Govindananda died at age 137. He had lived an incredibly strenuous life, actually journeying around the world by foot. Many heads of state were his friends, yet he lived humbly in a small jungle hut. When he became aware that it was time to die, he spoke quietly to a few disciples with him, gave a final blessing—"Live right life, worship God"—lay down, rested his head on his right palm in his usual sleeping position, and simply stopped breathing.

Wouldn't you like to die such a good death when your time comes? One of the remarkable things about saintly people is that even their deaths are often acts of inspiration and love. After showing us how to live—selflessly and in service to others—they show us how to die—fearlessly and with dignity, strong in faith to the end. Mahatma Gandhi trained himself well enough to have the name of God on his lips at the moment of death; Joan of Arc died saying the name of Christ.

We learn so much by example, by simply observing others and then trying to model our behavior after theirs. Inspiration begets imitation—a perfectly valid way to educate, and especially so with regard to death, when used consciously. That is because our fear of dying is, to a large extent, *unconscious* imitation. It is unconscious adoption of the emotional responses we observed in others when we were young. We saw people look sad over the death of a loved one and, although we didn't understand the response, we nevertheless were subtly conditioned to imitate the response. Movies, TV, books, and magazines reinforce it. Thus, part of our fear of dying is due to nothing more than modeling of widespread social behavior.

That's not to say grief is unjustified. But we must begin to distinguish the grief over loss of a loved one from the death-fear associated with it. Moreover, we must see that not every death of a loved one must *necessarily* elicit grief, as if we simply push a button to turn on the "crying machine" whenever we hear of a death. If someone is very old or has been incurably ill for some time, his death can be regarded as a blessing. There's no need for tears in such a situation—only fond memories. This is especially so in the case of saints, whose manner of passing is more a cause for rejoicing than grief. In this chapter, therefore, we are going to examine the deaths of holy people, revered spiritual figures and heroic personalities who demonstrated the elimination of death-fear in themselves. We are going to hear stories of how they spent their last hours. But we are going to do more than just listen. We are going to consciously project ourselves into the minds and bodies of these people. We are going to *become* them as they die, and learn by imitation as we experience "dying the good death."

Some of the following stories come from a useful book, *Philosophy of Death and Dying* by M.W. Kamath.° "To know how a man dies," Kamath writes, "is to know the man." And he illustrates his words with accounts of how many famous people have died.

Gautama Buddha, well into his eighties, continued teaching and preaching to the end. When he felt himself dying, he told his faithful disciple Ananda, who began to weep. The Buddha admonished him, "Have I not already,

°Available from the Himalayan International Institute, RD 1, Honesdale, PA 18431.

on former occasions, told you that it is the very nature of things that we must separate from them and leave them? The foolish man conceives the idea of 'self' [personal self or ego], the wise man sees there is no ground on which to build it!"

Disciples gathered around the Buddha and he delivered his Dying Sermon. He ended his farewell address with these words, "Behold now, brethren, I exhort you by saying: Decay is inherent in all component things, but the truth will remain forever! Work out your salvation with diligence." Those were his last words. Then the Buddha fell into deep meditation and entered nirvana.

St. Francis of Assisi, as his life neared its end, was taken to the palace of the Bishop of Assisi. A doctor was fetched to treat him. St. Francis, wanting to know how long he had to live, asked the doctor, who avoided a direct answer for some time but finally said that the disease was incurable and that he might die soon. St. Francis, overjoyed, raised his hands and cried, "Welcome, Sister Death!" He bade farewell to his friends and friars, and dictated some letters. A few days later, near to death, he asked the doctor to announce the arrival of Sister Death. "She will open for me the door of life," he explained. Then, following his instructions, the Franciscan brothers spread a coarse cloth on the ground, placed their mentor on it, and sprinkled him with dust and ashes. St. Francis was heard to mutter faintly the 142nd psalm. After that, he struggled to sing his own "Canticle of the Creatures," which contains these lines.

> And Death is our sister, we praise Thee for Death,
> Who releases the soul to the light of Thy gaze;
> And dying we cry with the last of our breath
> Our thanks and our praise.

But St. Francis' voice failed at that moment. He died singing the praise of death.

Sir Thomas More, English statesman and humanist, author of *Utopia*, the original "man for all seasons," was beheaded at 57. King Henry VIII, who split the Church

of England from the Roman Catholic Church, considered
More disloyal for not acknowledging him as true leader
of the church. Kamath tells us:

> On the day he was to be beheaded, he was led to the
> scaffold, still cheerful and still urbanely courteous to his
> guards. He leaned on the lieutenant of the guard as he
> climbed the scaffold. "I pray you," he told the unhappy
> guard, "see me safely up. As for my coming down, let me
> shift for myself." Ghoulish humor, but it showed the caliber
> of the man.
>
> Arriving at the top, somewhat out of breath, Sir Thomas
> embraced the thoroughly embarrassed executioner, paid
> him the customary gold coin and asked him to spare his
> beard, which he put outside the block, saying that certainly
> his beard had committed no treason to be so uncere-
> moniously cut off! Asked whether he had anything to say,
> Sir Thomas asked the assembled people to pray for him in
> this world and he would pray for them elsewhere. Then,
> in a magnificent gesture, he asked the people to pray
> earnestly for the king, that it might please God to give the
> king good counsel, protesting that he died the king's good
> servant, but God's first. And then the axe fell. It was the
> year 1535.

In his book *The Wheel of Death*, the Zen Buddhist
teacher Philip Kapleau tells us that many Zen masters
actually anticipated their "final" hour, meeting it with
equilibrium and even laughter, sometimes sitting in the
full crosslegged lotus posture or even, more rarely, standing on their heads. In fact, Kapleau says, the Zen masters
were so intimately involved with the *whole* of existence—
meaning they experienced life and death as an unbroken
continuum—that they found overinvolvement with any of
its parts, death included, to be a misplaced concern. "Why
do you want to know what will happen to you after you
die?" the Zen masters told inquiring disciples. "Find out
who you are now!"

Kapleau describes the death of Roshi (meaning "teacher")
Yamamoto. Almost blind at the age of 86 and no longer
able to teach or work in the monastery, this Zen master

decided it was time to die, so he stopped eating. When asked by his monks why he refused food, he replied that he had outlived his usefulness and was only a bother to everybody. They told him, apparently out of love for the old man, "If you die now when it is so cold, [it was January] everybody will be uncomfortable at your funeral and you will be an even greater nuisance, so please eat." Yamamoto thereupon resumed eating, but, Kapleau reports, when the weather warmed again he stopped, and not long after quietly toppled over and died.

Two other stories from *The Wheel of Death* are worth consideration here. The first concerns Master Etsugen. Shortly before he died, Etsugen called his monks together. It was December 1. "I've decided to die on the eighth of this month," he told them. "That's the day of the Buddha's enlightenment. If you have any questions left about the Teaching, you'd better ask them before then." The master continued with his regular duties during the next few days. Some of the monks therefore thought he was having a little fun at their expense. Most, however, were struck with grief at the imminent loss of their teacher.

On the evening of December 7, Etsugen assembled the monks and taught them for the last time about Buddha's enlightenment. Then he arranged his affairs and went into his room. At dawn, he took a bath, put on his ceremonial robes and, sitting erect in lotus posture, composed this death poem:

Shakyamuni [Buddha] descended the mountain.
I went up.
In my teaching, I guess I've always been
    something of a maverick.
And now I'm off to hell—yo ho!
The inquisitiveness of men is pure folly.

Then, shutting his eyes, and still sitting, he died.

The death of the Sixth Patriarch of Zen is equally moving. On the eighth day of the seventh month, Kapleau tells us, the master said to his monks, "Gather round me. I have decided to leave this world in the eighth month."

When the monks heard this they wept openly.

"For whom are you crying?" the master asked. "Are you worrying about me because you think I don't know where I'm going? If I didn't know, I wouldn't be able to leave you this way. What you're really crying about is that *you* don't know where I'm going. If you actually knew, you couldn't possibly cry because [you would be aware that] the True-nature is without birth or death, without going or coming. . . ."

On the day the master died he wrote a death verse and then said to the disciples,

Take good care of yourselves. I am going to leave you now. After I have left do not cry like people attached to the world. Do not accept condolences or money. Above all, do not wear mourning. It would not be in accordance with the correct Dharma [law of the universe] and you would be no disciples of mine if you did these things. Live as though I were still here. Do zazen [meditation] together. When there is calm, coming or going, right or wrong, and without abiding or departing, then that is the great Way. When I am gone, just practice correctly according to the Teaching, just as you did during my days with you. Remember, even were I to remain in this world, if you disobeyed my teaching, my presence among you would be pointless.

After saying this the master became silent. Suddenly at midnight, he entered nirvana. He was 76.

Karlis Osis and Erlendur Haraldsson, during their research into postmortem survival in India, found an extraordinary case of a yogi who, like Govindananda, died the good death. As they report it in *At the Hour of Death*:

A faculty member of a medical school in Benares described the death of his grandfather, who had practiced yoga. He was a philanthropist, having helped many persons in his vicinity, and was very religious. People came to him for a general uplift. In his case, the rise in mood [elevation of feelings] started forty-eight hours before death, which the doctor described as perfect consciousness with tranquility. He seemed to have a premonition of death, for which there were no sufficient medical reasons. He ordered a load of wood for the funeral pyre, sent a telegram to his son, and on the last day at four o'clock, asked the family members to eat something, since he would die at five thirty, and in accordance with Hindu custom, nobody would then be permitted to eat. The premonition came true, and he died at five thirty-five. He had performed Hindu purification procedures in order to prepare for death. He didn't show the slightest anxiety and was seen counseling relatives who were crying. He said to the weeping people, "You should be happy because I am going." He was perfectly controlled, unafraid, and tranquil. He described, step by step, how the body was dying. He told how his legs were becoming stiff and could be pricked without his feeling it, and how limb after limb was becoming numb and no longer a part of "the eternal self."

The Native American way of dying was described recently by Sun Bear, a Chippewa medicine man, and his medicine partner, Wabun. In their quarterly magazine *Many Smokes*,° they offered this account of how their tradition relates to death. Again I quote:

In the old way, when it was time to die, old ones would go off by themselves, feeling that the moment of death was as intimate between them and the Earth Mother as the moment of birth is between human mother and child. They would find a quiet place and there make prayers to the Great Spirit, thanking him for the life they had enjoyed. They would sing their song, and they would die.

There is a story of one old-timer who felt his time had come. He invited all of his friends to a gathering where they sang songs and made a feast. He had a big give-away, giving gifts to all his friends, telling them how happy he had been with their friendship. They, in turn, all spoke their good thoughts of him. Then, while they were singing songs, he closed his eyes and died. Many Indian people have been known to predict the exact date and time they would die.

°Available from the Bear Tribe Medicine Society, P.O. Box 9167, Spokane, WA 99209. It is now retitled *Wild Fire*.

Warrior societies used to let the old men go into battle one last time. When they went the young men would stand aside and say, "Let the old man count one last coup."

If people had lived a good, full life, then passing could be a good thing. Another Indian custom was to give away or make arrangements to give away everything a person had before he died. That way there was nothing for anyone to fight over after the person was gone. . . .

Like all other things in life, death is not permanent. It is but a change from one world, from one state of being into another. For those of us who learn to love life, with all of its changes, death should not be a fearful event. It should be a time of celebrating the continual evolution of the soul. When it is your time to pass, it should be with your mind wide open and your prayer in your heart. When one dear to you dies, besides sadness at your loss you should feel happiness that now the soul is free to soar to Kitche Manitou, the Great Spirit, our common Creator. Where there is love, there is no room for fear.

I'll close this chapter with a story about the death of the father of our country, George Washington. Again I'm indebted to M.V. Kamath for it. As he tells it, the general was in deep distress with labored breathing. After being put to bed, he told his aide, Tobias Lear,

I find I am going, my breath cannot continue long; I believed from the first attack it would be fatal; do you arrange and record all my late military letters and papers; arrange my accounts and settle my books, as you know more about them than anyone else. . . .

It was all very matter of fact, Kamath notes—no sentiment, no fear of death, no worry about either the past or the future.

In the late afternoon Washington was helped onto a chair so he could sit up. To the doctors standing by him he said, in a strained voice, "I feel myself going. I thank you for your attention. You had better not take any more trouble about me; but let me go off quietly; I cannot last long." Again there was calm acceptance of death. About 10 p.m. Lear noticed that Washington, who was back in bed, wished to speak, so he leaned close to hear what was being said.

With slightly blurred speech Washington told him, "Have me decently buried and do not let my body be put into a vault in less than two days after I am dead." Lear nodded, unable to speak, fighting to keep back tears. Washington looked at him directly and asked, "Do you understand me?"

"Yes, sir."

Washington spoke once more. " 'Tis well."

Mrs. Washington was keeping vigil by the foot of the bed. A little after ten, the general's breathing became much easier and he lay quietly. Lear still held his hand. Then, unexpectedly, Washington withdrew it to feel his own pulse. There was a change in his countenance. Washington's fingers slipped from his wrist and lay limp by his side. Doctor Craik laid his hand gently over Washington's eyes. There was no flicker. "Almost as if he realized that everything was now in readiness for his last command, George Washington withdrew in the presence of Death." It was a supreme study in self-control.

May these stories inspire you to cast out fear of dying.

12
Growing Old Gracefully: The Phenix Society

This chapter will describe an organization I'm associated with, the Phenix Society. I became part of it fourteen years ago because, after writing about it as a journalist, I sincerely felt it was doing valuable work in helping people to find meaning and direction in life. That includes dealing with the fear of dying. The Phenix Society was born in 1973 when a handful of southern Connecticut residents began to meet regularly in search of a positive approach to aging. They were all older people who'd been through a wide variety of life's shocks. Hobbies and weekly bridge games at the senior citizens' center weren't enough to satisfy them. They vaguely sensed there was a better way, but it wasn't until one of them read a passage in Carl Jung's *Modern Man in Search of a Soul* that the answer stood out clearly. Jung wrote,

> A human being would certainly not grow to be seventy or eighty years old if this longevity had no meaning for the species to which he belongs. . . . We cannot live the afternoon of life according to the program of life's morning.

That program is the all-too-common scramble for wealth, fame, status, power, sexual conquest, perhaps marriage with kids and a nice home—the usual game plans for youth. But sooner or later those game plans lose their luster. This generally happens between the ages of 35 and 50, statistically speaking—the time called midlife. Hence the term "midlife crisis," when apathy and depression can set in, with a loss of physical and mental vitality. "Old Mortality" starts to grin at you, and the Big Fear becomes prominent.

What's the answer? The development of wisdom. That alone is the intelligent way to deal with midlife crisis, as well as those later-life passages of pre-retirement stress, post-retirement doldrums, and that most profound transition of all, death.

The founders of the Phenix Society sensed vaguely what Jung said explicitly: If you try to live the second half of life the way you live the first, you end up mentally bankrupt, if not an alcoholic or a suicide. Pursuit of the usual materialistic goals and superficial values is simply unfulfilling for someone who has seen below the glitter. The buffeting these people had experienced was enough to deepen their perceptions beyond surface phenomena. So their weekly gatherings centered on the search for revitalized sense of purpose, direction and fulfillment. The format they developed was based on reading, discussion, and meditation. Their goal was wisdom and serenity.

Thus the Phenix Society was born—"Phenix" because it is the immemorial symbol of renewal. Today there are more than three dozen Phenix Clubs from coast to coast, with a total membership of several hundred. The clubs operate autonomously, sponsored by the parent organization, the Phenix Society, which is a nonprofit educational corporation chartered in Connecticut. It costs nothing to join and there are no dues.

Our introductory brochure describes the Phenix Society as "a friendship association of men and women who seek to improve the quality of their lives. The philosophical and spiritual requirements of the second half of life are its central concerns." What do we mean by "quality"? We mean the same exuberant sense of purpose, direction, and fulfillment that most people have in younger years as they pursue the usual materialistic goals. But this time the goals are based on higher values—such as growth to cosmic consciousness, a sense of responsibility for planetary management, and an intelligent preparation for death. There is much to tell about the Phenix Society, but this is not the place for the full story. Instead, I'll focus on how we view death.

The handbook we use, *The Club of Life** written by founder Jerome Ellison, describes twelve "conditions of being" which we've found to be useful guidelines for assisting members in their progress to joyful, creative victory over aging. The first condition reads: "We admit that death is closer for us who are in the second half of our lives than it is for the average person; that in this respect we are different from the majority of people." Death may be closer, but, we add, we no longer fear it. Or at least we are taking positive steps to deal with the fear. We recognize that it's one thing to discuss death intellectually as a remote, impersonal event, but it's quite another to accept death unemotionally when it's your own under examination. The Phenix approach provides *experiential* means for overcoming fear of dying.

First, there is the weekly meeting where open discussion encourages people to voice their fears and face them. This sharing of secret fears is not simply "letting it all hang out." For there are other members who have already dealt with that fear, to some degree, and who have hard-won wisdom to offer in response to the sharing. Thus, the weekly meetings are times of friendship when we give and receive, care as well as share, profiting from the experience of others. It is educational as well as cathartic.

> Death, that awful and mysterious thing we had heard about all our lives as a terrible but distant threat, is now near, actually reaching out its cold feelers to claim our bodies. And we cannot escape. What will come will come to us as it comes to everybody.

---

*Available from the Phenix Society, P.O. Box 351, Cheshire, CT 06410.

This admission and frank discussion of death-fear has the positive effect of an affirmation of life. The handbook describes what early Phenix Clubbers found:

Instead of telling ourselves we weren't showing any marked effects of aging, we began to own up to the fact that we were. Instead of pretending that we weren't really going to die very soon, we began to concede that our time was not so far off. Instead of pretending that we were just the same as the younger elements of the population, we began to accept the circumstance that in important ways we were different. Instead of rating youth as the "prime" of life, we cast aside the youth cult and its propaganda, in which we had been immersed all our lives, seeing youth as only one of several transitory phases of a complete life cycle and age as the culmination that gives both youth and age their meaning and fulfillment. Instead of fearing death as an ignoble end, we began to see that meeting it with serenity, courage, resourcefulness, and skill provides that crowning challenge of the fully lived life.

The results astonished us. Only when we gave them up did we begin to realize what a price in energy-expenditure the maintenance of our denial mechanisms had been exacting, what an enormous effort it is to try to live a lie. We took up with a will our therapy of affirmation. Yes, we were getting older and feebler. Yes, we would die statistically sooner than the younger elements of the population. Yes, we might be sick for a while before we died.

For some of us, these admissions were not easy at first. To admit is not the same as shallow intellectual acknowledgement. To admit is to "let in," to take into the very structure of our being the same facts we had taken such exhaustive pains to keep out. . . .

But we found that if we stuck with it, and utilized all available supports, we would win through to a point where we could calmly (or with only brief moments of panic!) consider our approaching death as one of the ordinary facts of life. Our fears diminished to a point where they stimulated rather than inhibited constructive action.

And now some amazing things began to happen. As the energy we had been pouring into denial mechanisms was released, new resources of mental, physical and emotional vigor came pouring into us. We were almost "ourselves" again. As we directed our imaginative powers away from morbidity, they took hold of the problems of the last third of life with surprising skill. Answers to formerly unanswerable problems began to appear, sometimes with unexpected ease. Were our physical and mental power diminished? Very well, we'd put to the best possible use whatever was left of them. Were we going to die before long? Then we'd better pull ourselves together to do a good job of it. As we began to look around with open eyes, we found worlds of resources opening to us we had never known existed. Why, the last third of life might be a really splendid thing! With a new will, we began to explore life's new possibilities.

In addition to a weekly discussion, members are encouraged to pursue a reading program at home on their own. Not all of it focuses on death, of course, but there is a solid list of titles that we recommend for use in exploring your attitude toward death and in examining the evidence of postmortem survival.

Last of all, there is meditation. The Twelve Conditions state that meditation is an integral part of the Phenix approach to living harmoniously and creatively. Since I've already discussed meditation in Chapter 9, I'll simply say here that members are encouraged to meditate regularly every day because of its demonstrated value in reducing death-fear and opening up the mind to new dimensions of being—joyful, creative dimensions—that more and more pervade one's entire way of living.

The Phenix Society's approach, then, is based on reading, discussion, and meditation. We say that the courage to face death—your own death—is indeed teachable. Nor is it courage based on false hopes. It springs from the very fabric of ultimate reality. Death-fear can be allayed intellectually, emotionally, experientially. As Phenix Society members, we aim to grow to cosmic consciousness in the company of supportive friends who look on death as a great adventure. And although the original intent of the organization was to meet the needs of people in the last third of life, we've found that young people are also seeking to travel in our company, so we've welcomed them. Thus, there is no age limit. Such wisdom as we have is there for everyone, and freely shared.°

°For more information, write to: The Phenix Society, P.O. Box 351, Cheshire, CT 06410.

13

Planning Intelligently for Your Demise

The basic intent of funeral observances is unclear. On the one hand, they function to expedite the departure of the deceased and his presumed adjustment to a new existence. But, on the other hand, they function equally to prepare the mourners for their own ultimate demise.

Roger W. Wescott,
"Death and Culture," in *Voices*

Death comes every 18 seconds in America, according to the U.S. Department of Commerce. That means about 2,000,000 deaths each year. Nearly 23,000 morticians handle the funeral arrangements at a total expense of more than $6.4 billion. Add to that figure the cost of medical care for the dying in hospitals and convalescent homes, and you can see that a major industry is built around death and dying in America. Isn't it surprising, then, that so many people know so little about how to handle the legal, financial, medical, and ceremonial aspects of it? More often than not, survivors are thrust into a situation where large sums of money are involved, yet they have only the vaguest notion of what to do. Moreover, they are generally so grief-stricken that they cannot adequately perform the necessary functions.

A recent Federal Trade Commission investigation of "the high cost of dying" found that the average funeral and burial costs more than $2,500, making it the third most

111

expensive purchase many consumers make—after a house and a car. Nearly two decades ago, Jessica Mitford pointed this out powerfully in her best-selling book, *The American Way of Death*, which told of people being sold needlessly expensive and elaborate services when their loved ones died. "Choice," she wrote, "doesn't enter the picture for the average individual faced, generally for the first time, with the necessity of buying a product of which he is totally ignorant, at a moment when he is least in a position to quibble." She called funerals in America "a fantastic array of costly merchandise and services . . . pyramided to dazzle the mourners and facilitate the plunder of the next of kin."

This chapter will show you an intelligent way to prepare for your own demise, and will have you actually begin those preparations. In your doing so, you will become even further accustomed to the idea of personal death. You will also be performing an act of love and consideration for those eventually left behind because you will have acted in advance to reduce their burden of grief and responsibilities at the time of your death.

A number of books offer pragmatic advice on what preparations should be made and how far in advance they should be carried out. Your will, for example, should be made even when you are young, and it should be reviewed every five or ten years. A will is a contract with death. Because of that, many people avoid making one, but you should face the situation squarely. If you die intestate— without a will—state and federal taxes can take a much larger bite of your property than you'd like, leaving less of an estate for your spouse, family, friends, and favorite charities. Wills can also be used to leave instructions about funeral proceedings, including—as I suggested in Chapter 8—use of a videotape conveying the deceased's last words. It's therefore not simply an act of courage to make a will; it's also an act of love.

Some people buy a cemetery plot at an early age because they realize that, like almost everything else, the price will continue to rise. Not only is it possible to plan your own funeral, you can also pay for it before you die. Both funeral preplanning and prepayment are endorsed by consumer organizations such as the American Association of Retired Persons and the Washington, D.C. based Continental Association of Funeral Memorial Societies. An AARP official, Patricia Hoath, told syndicated columnist Cheryl Jensen that preplanning should be done out of consideration for the loved ones left behind, since so many decisions must be made at the time of your death. "Everyone should sit down with their spouse and their children and talk about the funeral arrangements they want," Hoath said, adding that the best thing is to put your desires in writing, make several copies, and distribute them to everyone who will be involved, from the family to the funeral home. This not only can ease the inevitable grief at your passing; it can also reduce the cost of dying, since prefinanced funeral plans allow time for comparison shopping, and the fee is paid in pre-inflation dollars. You can get valuable advice on conventional funerals and low cost alternatives in *Funerals: Consumer's Last Rights* by the editors of *Consumer Reports*. Write to: Book Department, A107, Consumers Union, Orangeburg, NY 10962.

Another useful guide is the brief booklet, *Pre-Planning the Funeral—Why? Who? How?* This free four-page publication is offered by the Consumer Information Bureau of the National Selected Morticians, 1616 Central Street, Evanston, IL 60201. The first paragraph states:

> The contemplation of one's own death and its effect on one's family is a necessary part of life. It is both wholesome and wise to acknowledge the inevitable and consider that which may reasonably be anticipated. It is only in such degree as we accept death as a part of life that we are able to fully live.

The booklet further advises that planning your own funeral requires care, consideration, competent counseling and a full awareness of the consequences. "How your planning could, or would, affect the actions and reactions of you and your family goes beyond the purely practical, such as in drawing a will or providing insurance." There is a long two-page form included in the booklet entitled "Suggestions to Those Who Plan My Funeral." It comprehensively covers the various aspects of a normal funeral, and you will do well to read it for an overview. Even so, as the first page warns,

> No form of questionnaire, including the one attached, should ever be used as a "do-it-yourself" funeral kit. Nor is this booklet totally adequate and complete in itself. Before you make final plans you need conferences, counseling, and complete knowledge . . . there can be no satisfactory substitute for these essentials.

With that prudent counsel in mind, you can nevertheless fill out the questionnaire on pp. 116-7 (which I obtained from my local memorial society) for both intellectual and emotional reasons. Intellectually speaking, the experience of considering these aspects of your eventual death will help you to plan more intelligently for it. Emotionally speaking, you are again confronting fear as an exercise similar to those you conducted in Chapter 8. From both points of view, it is therefore *practical*—just as this book's title states—to provide the personal data sought in the questionnaire.

The best publication I've found on these and related matters is *A Manual of Death Education and Simple Burial* by Ernest Morgan. Since its first edition in 1962 it has sold several hundred thousand copies. A review of it in *The Whole Earth Catalog* says that in 64 pages it quietly tells you how to avoid "the ghastly system of converting human leftovers into products packaged as 'funerals.' In simple language backed by intelligent sympathy, it suggests ways to surround the *act* of passage with appropriate *rites* of passage that offer real meaning to people in need of meaning." The manual is available for $2.50 from Celo Press, Route 5, Burnsville, NC 28714.

Because the manual states that it is happy to be quoted and that it welcomes reprints not to exceed five pages (so long as proper credit is given, as I've done above), I'm going to base the rest of this chapter on *A Manual of Death Education and Simple Burial*. It won't be a long chapter because the 64 pages of the manual tell the story better. I therefore urge you to buy a copy. Here are some highlights of it to serve as reasons why.

There are four parts to the manual: Death Education, About Funeral and Memorial Societies, Simple Burial and Cremation, and How the Dead Can Help the Living. Each is packed with the most practical and far-sighted advice you can ever hope to find on this subject.

Part One, Death Education, discusses it as preparation for living. It gives facts, philosophy, counsel, and moving personal accounts. The section entitled "On Dying at Home" is a good example. I quote in part:

> Hospitals are geared to saving lives—not letting them go. Home is generally a nicer place in which to die, if the necessary arrangements can be made for the patient's care. This is particularly true for patients who, together with their families, have been able to accept their approaching death. Further, I can say from experience that the problems of home-care, when actually tackled, may prove less formidable than they seemed in prospect. . . .

It then notes that some insurance benefits require hospitalization, thus preventing people from dying at home, even though the costs are generally lower. The solution?

> One way to approach this problem is to inquire of one's insurance company at a time when there is no need in prospect, as to whether and under what conditions their coverage will apply to home-care. Another way is to ask, when the need occurs, if they will cover home-care or will insist on the generally more costly procedure of hospitalization. A hospital chart carefully kept and signed at regular intervals by an MD or an RN (with the letters after the name) plus an accurate expense record (including receipts) can sometimes meet the requirements for insurance benefits for home-care.

The section on Death Education also discusses: relating to a dying person, dealing with grief, viewing the remains,

Statement for the Guidance of My Family in the Event of My Death

Personal Data

Name _____ Address _____

Date and Place of Birth _____ Home Phone _____

Occupation _____ Are you retired? Yes ___ No ___

Social Security Number _____ Ever in Armed Services? Yes ___ No ___

If yes, give Dates and Serial No. _____ Unit or Ship _____

Name of Father _____ His Birthplace _____

Maiden name of Mother _____ Her Birthplace _____

Your marital status: Married _____ Never Married _____ Widowed _____ Divorced _____

If married, widowed or divorced, give maiden name of wife or husband _____

Next of Kin: Name and Address _____

Name and Address _____

Instructions for Funeral Arrangements

(Read Guidebook before filling in this section)

A. I prefer the simple, inexpensive final arrangements described in the Guidebook as:

☐ PLAN I   Limited calling hours and funeral service.

☐ PLAN II   Funeral service, but no calling hours at funeral home.

☐ PLAN III   Private burial, followed by memorial service.

☐ PLAN IV   Cremation, followed by memorial service.

I request my family not to spend more than $ _____ on my funeral arrangements.

B. Services: Religious and Memorial.

☐ I prefer that the Funeral Service, or Memorial Service, be held at: (Give Name and address of Church, Synagogue, Home or Chapel)

_____

I wish the Service to be conducted by _____

I request that during the Service: ☐ The Casket be closed.

☐ The Casket be covered with a pall.

I request the following Music and Readings be included in the Service: _____

_____

C.   ☐ Flowers may be sent. ☐ I prefer not to have Flowers.

☐ I hope that instead of Flowers, Gifts may be made to the _____

☐ I prefer that there be no Religious or Memorial Service.

Disposal of the Body.

☐ I prefer Burial in the following Cemetery _____, Registered in the Name of _____

In Lot No. _____, Section No. _____

The Deed to the Lot is located _____

Description of Grave Marker or Monument desired _____

☐ I prefer Cremation: ☐ Prior to a Memorial Service. ☐ After Funeral Service. ☐ I wish to have my ashes: ☐ Scattered by

Funeral Director (Special Instructions _____);

☐ Placed in Container and Buried in accordance with Burial Instructions above; ☐ Handled in accordance with the wishes of my family.

☐ I prefer to have my body donated for the purpose of Medical Research.

☐ I wish to donate my Eyes to the Eye Bank for Sight Restoration.

D.   ☐ I prefer the following Funeral Director _____

I have made the following advance arrangements with this Director _____

_____

_____

_____

Signed _____

Date _____

how death ceremonies serve human needs, role playing in death education, and many other topics. It concludes with a list of resources for death education: books, periodicals, and where to get bibliographies on the subject.

Part Two, About Funeral and Memorial Societies, tells how they work, where they are located, what they cost, and how to join one. A directory of funeral and memorial societies belonging to the Continental Association of Funeral & Memorial Societies and the Memorial Society Association of Canada is included.

Basically, these groups provide alternatives to the usual funeral. They are, the manual states, a voluntary, non-profit association of people which was formed to obtain dignity, simplicity, and economy in funeral arrangements through advance planning. A memorial society is managed by an unpaid board of directors chosen from the membership and supported by a one-time or annual fee from members. The fee ranges from $6 to $20.

Even if you wish to have a funeral home carry out your instructions, rather than a memorial society, it is wise to read this section and to personally investigate your local society. The information you'll get could save you hundreds of dollars because you'll learn, for example, that embalming is not legally required in most states if burial or cremation is carried out within 48 hours. Many funeral homes regularly carry out this "service" at profitable fees because the family is unaware that it is not necessary. (Some may even try to persuade you, if you object, that it has cosmetic value and shows greater "respect" for the deceased. These tactics have rightly outraged the consumer movement, but unless you carefully investigate, you'll probably leave your survivors with an inflated—but avoidable—bill for "expenses.")

Part Three, Simple Burial and Cremation, contains specific directions for how to obtain simplicity, dignity, and economy in funeral arrangements through advance planning—with or without a society. The topics discussed include: financial resources at the time of death, funeral prepayment plans, advice on how to deal with funeral directors (don't call them undertakers), do-it-yourself funerals, cremation, legal expenses at the time of death, and other aspects of advance planning.

A useful "Checklist of Things to Be Done" when death occurs is also to be found in this section. I am reproducing it in full here to help you in considering all aspects of your own death, and especially in preparing intelligently for it.

Checklist of Things to Be Done When a Death Occurs

Assuming that the family belongs to a memorial society and that the matters above [i.e., discussed in the manual] have been taken care of, there still remain numerous details, many of which can be taken care of by friends though others require the attention of the family. Scratch off the items in the following checklist which do not apply; check the others as they are taken care of:

☐ Decide on time and place of funeral or memorial service(s).

☐ Make list of immediate family, close friends and employer or business colleagues. Notify each by phone.

☐ If flowers are to be omitted, decide an appropriate memorial to which gifts may be made. (As a church, library, school or some charity.)

☐ Write obituary. Include age, place of birth, cause of death, occupation, college degrees, memberships held, military service, outstanding work, list of survivors in immediate family. Give time and place of services. Deliver in person, or phone, to newspapers.

☐ Notify insurance companies, including automobile insurance for immediate cancellation and available refund.

☐ Arrange for members of family or close friends to take turns answering door or phone, keeping careful record of calls.

☐ Arrange appropriate child care.

☐ Coordinate the supplying of food for the next days.

☐ Consider special needs of the household, as for cleaning, etc., which might be done by friends.

☐ Arrange hospitality for visiting relatives and friends.

☐ Select pall bearers and notify. (Avoid men with heart or back difficulties, or make them honorary pall bearers.)

☐ Notify lawyer and executor.

☐ Plan for disposition of flowers after funeral (hospital or rest home?)

☐ Prepare copy for printed notice if one is wanted.

☐ Prepare list of persons to receive acknowledgments of flowers, calls, etc. Send appropriate acknowledgments. (Can be written notes, printed acknowledgments, or some of each.)

☐ Check carefully all life and casualty insurance and death benefits, including Social Security, credit union, trade union, fraternal, military, etc. Check also on income for survivors from these sources.

☐ Check promptly on all debts and installment payments. Consult with creditors and ask for more time before the payments are due.

☐ If deceased was living alone, notify utilities and landlord and tell post office where to send mail. Take precaution against thieves.

The last part of *A Manual of Death Education and Simple Burial* tells how the dead can help the living. "If we truly accept our own mortality and genuinely identify ourselves with humanity, we will gladly help in every way we can," it states, noting that many lives can be saved, and health and sight restored to thousands, through the intelligent "salvaging" of organs and tissues. In addition, medical and dental training requires thousands of bodies each year for anatomical study by future doctors and dentists. Last of all, medical research needs cooperation in the form of permission for autopsies and the bequeathal of special parts, such as earbones of people with hearing difficulties.

All these matters are discussed succinctly, and the names and addresses of appropriate organizations are listed for those who want information or the necessary forms. Since, in Chapter 5, you said goodbye to your body and watched it "moulderin' in the grave," by now you should be able to consider the topics discussed in the manual's Part Four with little anxiety. Moreover, if you think of the gladness and gratitude someone will feel for restoring his or her sight, hearing, or other function, surely this will help to reduce anxiety even further. Even in death you'll be needed and loved—by someone unknown to you!

14
Helping Yourself by Helping Others—Volunteer Organizations for the Dying

If you deal with the dying, they will give you life.
Ancient folk wisdom

What can we expect when the prospect of our own deaths has changed from a distant possibility to a present probability? This year, 75% of us who die in the United States will end our days in hospitals or nursing homes. We can expect unfamiliar surroundings and procedures, intense, conflicting feelings, and inadequate support for our very real emotional needs. There are many reasons for this grim picture. Among them is the culture in which we live. This culture teaches us to deny death and the dying while it has made available to us great technological and medical advancements which prolong the time of our living and our dying. Many therapeutic treatments offer us precious time in which to come to terms with our deaths, the feelings we are experiencing and the relationships important to us—time to share our fear, sorrow, love and growth. Yet this gift can weigh heavily when offered by a culture that insists upon ignoring the psychological realities of dying. Many of us will be left alone in our fear and will have no one with whom to share our last days.

The Shanti Project is one hope for change toward a different scenario for the dying.

Shanti is a Sanskrit word which means peace—the inner peace that passeth understanding. The Shanti Project, whose newsletter is quoted above, is a San Francisco Bay area counseling service that offers caring, on-going support to patients and families facing life-threatening illness. Completely nonprofit and volunteer-staffed, it was organized in 1975 by Dr. Charles Garfield, whom I mentioned in Chapter 9.

Early in Garfield's work as a clinical research psychologist at the Cancer Research Institute in San Francisco, he met Larry, 20, an ex-Marine, who was to be his initial encounter with a dying patient. Through his relations with Larry and his family, Garfield was forced to confront fears about his own death. The patient became the teacher as Garfield opened himself emotionally to the situation. During the time he dealt with the fear, loneliness, and pain Larry was experiencing, Garfield kept a journal of the process. Actually, Larry had suggested he do so in order that his "story" might be used to teach other healthcare professionals. A few days before Larry died, he looked at Garfield and said with surprising intensity for a person whose body was black and blue, with sunken eyes and yellow skin, "I have something very important to say . . . Dying alone is not easy."

As he continued to work with the dying, Garfield became aware that hospital personnel often experienced as much fear and denial of death as did the dying themselves. For in addition to their anxiety about personal extinction, they also saw the dying as a threat to their professional status as healers. Death meant they had "failed." Thus, they tended to withdraw, spending less time with the dying than with other patients, and depersonalizing them by treating them as objects rather than human beings. Caring and communication were terribly absent. It all remained at a biomedical level. Hospitals, it seemed, were not very hospitable. As one elderly man dying of lung cancer stated, "I'll be damned if I'll share my feelings about death and dying with anyone who makes two-minute U-turns at the foot of my bed."

Nor could the dying talk easily about their feelings with family, friends, and relatives. They, too, were ignorant about death, and afraid. Intimate feelings were blocked, compounding the plight of the dying by isolation. The dying, their families, the healthcare professionals—all needed help of a special kind, Garfield saw. Along with others who shared his concern, he began to search for a means of dealing with the emotional needs of people facing life-threatening illness. Stewart Brand, of *Whole Earth Catalog* fame, suggested that a group of volunteers who had the interest, ability, and time to work with the dying could be organized and reached at a central number. The volunteers could be matched with clients whose needs they were best equipped to meet, and then go out into the community to visit with clients wherever support was needed.

Thus it began. In February 1975 the Shanti telephone line was installed at a Berkeley address and 14 volunteer counselors responded to calls for assistance. Today there are more than 400 trained volunteers, 65 staff, and a $2.9 million budget providing free information service to approximately 2,000 people monthly nationwide. In 1984 the focus of the Shanti Project shifted to the AIDS epidemic, and now it is dedicated exclusively to people with AIDS and their loved ones in San Francisco County. It offers various programs for emotional, informational, recreational and practical support, along with public education and referral services. Despite its local focus, its training facilitators coordinate out-of-town training for many U.S. cities and have even trained people in other nations. Its video training materials have been distributed widely; a sample tape is available to give you a preview feel for the contents of the other videotapes.

The art of being fully present as a willing companion to a dying person is not easily developed, but learning it can be a powerful opportunity for personal growth and resolution of your own death-fear. Since Shanti-like groups are springing up around the country, you have a chance to help yourself by helping others—as a volunteer in an organization for the dying. The rest of this chapter describes six other organizations that exist to offer various kinds of humane care to the dying. Their addresses and telephone numbers are listed at the end of the chapter.

National Hospice Organization

Hospice, a word familiar from the Middle Ages, means "shelter for the traveller." Originally provided by religious orders for pilgrims, these communities for sojourners broadened their mission to include care for the sick and wounded. Today the name describes a form of treatment designed to give comfort to the terminally ill and their families.

The hospice approach honors the dying. It helps them face death without pain or fear, and makes no attempt to cure or prolong life. In addition to medical care, it offers fellowship, not only to the patient, but to his family unit as well. In fact, hospice philosophy makes the *family* the primary unit of care. As one hospice member put it, a hospice adds life to your years, not years to your life.

For human beings, dying—like birthing—is a social process as well as a biological one, and therefore is best carried out with assistance. Hospices provide that assistance, that hospitality. The modern hospice, writes Sandol Stoddard in her useful 1978 survey, *The Hospice Movement*, is different from the hospital.

> It is the difference in the quality of human life assumed and provided for, that makes for the contrast. . . . People in hospices are not attached to machines, nor are they manipulated by drips or tubes, or by the administration of drugs that cloud the mind without relieving pain. Instead, they are given comfort by methods sometimes rather sophisticated but often amazingly simple and obvious; and they are helped to live fully in an atmosphere of loving kindness and grace until the time has come for them to die a natural death. It is a basic difference in attitudes about the meaning and value of human life, and about the

significance of death itself, which we see at work in the
place called *hospice*.

According to a 1979 *Los Angeles Times* article about
hospices, a mutual respect is built up by talking and touch-
ing between staff and patient. Family may visit at any hour
of the day or night. Patients can bring their favorite objects
to their bedside, such as pictures, vases, pillows, and
bedspreads.

Hospice care need not be carried out in a special building. Although there are hospices within some hospitals
(e.g., St. Luke's in New York, Highland Park in Chicago),
the hospice movement in America can list only a few
hospice programs that function in buildings specially for
them, such as Riverside Hospice in New Jersey, Hillhaven
Hospice in Tucson, and Kaiser-Permanente Hospice near
Los Angeles. All the rest are home-care programs, reports
the National Hospice Organization, headquarters in
America for the hospice movement. There are more than
1,700 hospice programs actually providing home care
now. The largest hospice in America, founded by The
Connecticut Hospice, Inc. of New Haven is in nearby
Branford, Connecticut, with 44 inpatient beds, a day care
center, an outpatient program and headquarters for the
home care staff.

Because no expensive drugs, therapies, or machines
are used to try to effect a cure, and because lay workers
are also used alongside medical staff, hospices are less
expensive than hospitals—about one-third cheaper.
Home-care reduces the cost even more. According to
Stoddard, "Home care by New Haven's hospice has been
shown to cost, on the average, about $450 over a three-
month period." She adds, "The hospice achievement is . . . a
cause for general celebration. It is one of the rare events
in our time which is both fiscally creative and morally
sound."

Volunteers play a large part in hospice functioning. At
the Connecticut Hospice, Inc., an adjunct organization
entitled The Hospice Institute for Education, Training
and Research has spun off recently. Its purpose: "To

educate, train, and conduct research based on the Hospice concept and philosophy; to achieve the highest quality of life possible for the terminally ill and their families."

This is where you can come in. In announcing the Institute, its first executive director, Dennis Rezendes, told the *New Haven Register* that the training program "amounts to a formal structuring of what has in a sense been already going on for some time—people coming in to the Hospice headquarters for meetings where they can find out about what we are doing, and take it back to their hospice-type projects in whatever part of the country."

The Institute's goals, the article stated, include "changing attitudes toward needs of the terminally ill and their families. Hospice puts several things ahead of simply prolonging biological life, such as maximum freedom from pain, spiritual well-being—and informing the public as to the needs and how to meet them." Another goal will be increasing the level of skills of all care-givers and enlarging their sense of values as they relate to patients and their families. To do so, courses lasting from one to five days are offered to the public. For information, write to the Hospice Institute.

No one ever said dying was easy, the National Hospice Organization brochure states. But for those dying from terminal illness, and for their families, the growing hospice movement has brought new hope and meaning. It offers the same to you as a volunteer. The need exists, the training is available. The next move is up to you.

The Dying Project

The Dying Project was established in 1977 by the well-known American yogi, Ram Dass, author of *Be Here Now* and other books describing his spiritual exploration. His colleague, Stephen Levine, assisted and is director of the project. It is one of several service-oriented projects being carried out under the auspices of the Hanuman Foundation, which Ram Dass also established. The first newsletter of the Dying Project made a clear distinction between its efforts and those of Hospice and similar healthcare-oriented humanitarian organizations. While declaring that the Dying Project honors and supports these endeavors, Ram Dass said:

> We must make . . . clear at the outset that this is not the major thrust of our project. We recognize that life is primarily a vehicle for spiritual awakening, and thus dying, being a part of living, must also fulfill that function. Thus, we are exploring the way in which dying serves that process of spiritual awakening. For both the person who is dying and those in attendance, the experience is potentially the *most* significant opportunity for awakening of a lifetime. . . .
>
> Succinctly, then, we might say that this project is concerned with awakening through dying. By belaboring the above distinction, we hope in the long run to avoid confusion and to attract to our work particularly those people who see their awakening as the primary reason for both their life and their death.

The Dying Project limits itself to newsletters, lectures, tapes, a book entitled *A Gradual Awakening*, special retreats, and a free consultation phone for the terminally ill and those working closely with death (telephone 505-758-1181). The Project also is setting up a Dying Center (which will get underway soon). The retreats include both discussion and direct exploration through meditation of attitudes, reactions and possibilities relating to the processes of dying and death. As the newsletter puts it, "Investigation of the moment-to-moment birth and death of the mind, the death of the temporal body and, most importantly, the death of the separate self will be accomplished with the aid of basic Buddhist mindfulness meditation (vipassana) and guided meditation, as well as deep personal work through group process and individual sharings." The Hanuman Foundation Tape Library offers useful and very inexpensive cassette tapes of Ram Dass speaking on various occasions about death and dying, conscious dying, guided meditations, inspirational stories, and answering audience questions. The Dying Project newsletters offer practical instruction in death meditation and inspirational/educational articles and quotations. I offer a few excerpts from Stephen Levine's *A Gradual Awakening*, as quoted in the second newsletter:

> In the course of teaching meditation with Elisabeth Kübler-Ross, she asked me to visit some of her dying patients. Very soon, it became clear that working with the dying was a means of working on myself. . . .
>
> I know very few people who work with the dying who aren't deeply affected and often fatigued by it. It is very demanding work. Only when we can see life and death as not so separate, as part of an ongoing process of maturation, of coming home, of returning to God, of returning to the sources—whatever terms we try to define this process with—can we stay mindful of the context in which the pain and dying is occurring. Then working with someone who's in pain, we honor their difficulty, we see how difficult it is for them, but we don't reinforce their resistance to that pain by saying how awful pain is and therefore intensify their affliction. . . .
>
> A person's in the room with me and he's very close to dying and afraid. I can feel the fear of death in myself. In working through my fear, I give him an opportunity, silent though it may be, to work through his. . . .
>
> Working with the dying is like facing a finely polished, very fierce mirror of my own reality. Because I see my fears, and how much I dislike pain. The conditioned dislike of pain, of uncomfortable mental and physical states, is very great—it's going to be something we're working with much of the time. . . .
>
> The attachment which wants someone to die some other way than the way he is dying is of no use to him; that's my problem. I learned not to bring my problems into another person's room; he's got problems of his own. I learned not to make someone else die my death for me. . . .
>
> Sometimes I'm with a person, and I'm stuck, and I just have to say, "I'm stuck now." And that's more honesty than that person may experience all day in a hospital. There's a lot of pretense in hospital rooms. The person lying in bed is often pretending, the people visiting are pretending. My

work in that room is simply one of being. No pretense. And to be, I must be present. I have to be able to accept all of myself. And part of me is suffering and lying in that bed. My friend Bernard says, "When someone is dying, and you're sitting by the bed, there are two deaths occurring right then." And that, hopefully, is how it is.

The Elisabeth Kübler-Ross Center

No one has done more than Dr. Elisabeth Kübler-Ross to change medical attitudes toward death. At Head Waters, Virginia, she has established her own nonprofit organization, Shanti Nilaya, which is Sanskrit for "Home of Peace." Her passion is to educate members of the healing arts and the lay public about her conviction that death provides the key to the meaning of human existence and life itself. As she put it in the concluding chapter of *Death, The Final Stage of Growth*:

> There is no need to be afraid of death. It is not the end of the physical body that should worry us. Rather, our concern must be to *live* while we're alive—to release our inner selves from the spiritual death that comes with living behind a facade designed to conform to external definitions of who and what we are. Every individual human being born on this earth has the capacity to become a unique and special person unlike any who has ever existed before or will ever exist again. But to the extent that we become captives of culturally defined role expectations and behaviors—stereotypes, not ourselves—we block our capacity for self-actualization. We interfere with becoming all that we can be.
>
> Death is the key to the door of life. It is through accepting the finiteness of our individual existences that we are enabled to find the strength and courage to reject those extrinsic roles and expectations and to devote each day of our lives—however long they may be—to growing as fully as we are able.

A few paragraphs later she remarks:

> Humankind will survive only through the commitment and involvement of individuals in their own and others' growth

and development as human beings. This means development of loving and caring relationships in which all
members are as committed to the growth and happiness of
the others as they are to their own. Through commitment
to personal growth individual human beings will also make
their contribution to the growth and development—the
evolution—of the whole species to become all that human-
kind can and is meant to be. Death is the key to that
evolution. For only when we understand the real meaning
of death to human existence will we have the courage to
become what we are destined to be.

A brochure says the Center is dedicated to "the promo-
tion of the concept of unconditional love as an attainable
ideal. Our purpose is to spread knowledge and understanding of this concept with its underlying premises: 1) as
we accept full responsibility for all of our feelings, thoughts,
actions and choices, 2) as we, in a safe environment, release
negative emotions that we repressed in the past, we can
live free, happy, and loving lives, at peace with ourselves
and others. Our goal is to live this message and to spread it
far and wide. We believe that as individuals hear, experience the truth of this message, and live it themselves,
all of life will become increasingly rich in the values all
people inherently cherish."

Thus, from Kübler-Ross' original emphasis, as the title
of her bestseller proclaims, *On Death and Dying*, she has
come to emphasize life and living as the proper context
in which to consider your eventual demise. The Center
reaches out from Virginia through "Life, Death and Transition" workshops which Kübler-Ross and her staff conduct
at various locations around the United States. The workshops are five-day live-in experiences. The terminally ill
and parents of dying children are encouraged to attend,
along with people from a variety of cultural, religious,
and professional backgrounds.

Clear Light Society

"The practice of meditation is ultimately the *only* exercise with any degree of significance for learning to die

without fear," Patricia Shelton told me. Founder-Director of the Clear Light Society in Boston, she described the society's work in an interview.

The Clear Light Society has both service and educational objectives. First and foremost, it exists to assist the dying, not only in months or weeks prior to death, but at the time of death itself. "The assistance a person receives at the moment of death is very crucial," Shelton said. "It's not just a matter of sitting there meditating with the person. We *do* things—quite specific things—to keep the patient in the state of what we call 'profound relaxation, peaceful heart and clear mind.'"

What are those specific things? They are available in *Clear Light Practices for the Dying*, a unique training manual written by Shelton in which she gives exact instructions of what to do and what to say, moment by moment, as the dying person makes his or her transition. The manual is only for students of hers, but a book, *The Tale of the Mouse*, is for everyone and is obtainable through the Society.

Clear Light Society training requires several years. It begins with a weekend which presents the Society's mode of operation, giving both parties—the Society and prospective practitioners—a chance to look over one another. Those who go on register for a six-month initial training period, which introduces the principles of operation and some of the practices themselves. About twenty-five people are presently in different stages of the training.

Another objective of the Society is to inform the public about its existence and function. I asked Shelton to describe the origin of the Society. She replied,

The bulk of my teachings come from a certain Tibetan Buddhist lineage. As a matter of fact, it was a Tibetan teacher, Choygam Trungpa Rinpoche, who pointed out that this was my life's work about 18 years ago. I've also received teachings of enormous significance from a Zen master, Seung Sahn. Then from the Hindu tradition, I've had very intensive studies with Swami Muktananda. Rabbi Arnold Fein is my teacher on Jewish matters. A Jesuit priest, Father Richard Hunt, has instructed me on Roman

Catholic matters. And I have ministers and priests from other traditions who are also very accessible for me.

Thus, the Clear Light Society accommodates people from all walks of life and all religious backgrounds. The heart of the Society's work is what Shelton described as "a particular kind of meditation which I've developed with the assistance of my teachers over a period of years. I use that as a sort of substratum of all my work. And then I apply it to all the world's religions—to their doctrinal materials." She added, "That way the patient uses familiar materials, but in a wholly new way. They are not likely to feel strange with it, and therefore it is far more effective than being introduced to something that seems foreign. But the techniques need not be explicitly religious. It's for non-sectarian use also. It's for the terminally ill of all religions or no religion."

The Society also works with the family of the dying patient. The program is designed to give emergency training to family members in the skills necessary to assist the dying relative into a peaceful state, and is tailored to the religious belief system of the family, whether Christian, Jewish, or other. No charges of any kind are made by the Society to the dying or their families. There are fees for practitioner training, but they are geared to one's income.

The Hemlock Society

The Hemlock Society, a Los Angeles-based membership organization, believes in "active voluntary euthanasia for the terminally ill." A brochure says it seeks to promote a climate of public opinion which is tolerant of the right of hopelessly ill people to end their own lives in a planned manner. At the same time it approves of the work of those involved in suicide prevention and does not encourage suicide for any primary emotional, traumatic, or financial reasons in the absence of terminal illness. Contrary views held by other religions and philosophies are respected by Hemlock. "The final decision to terminate life is ultimately one's own. Hemlock believes this action, and most of all its timing, to be an extremely personal decision, whenever possible taken in concert with family, close friends and personal physician."

Hemlock has published a book, *Let Me Die Before I Wake* by Derek Humphrey, which contains detailed case histories of suicide.

Concern for Dying

The concept of a "Living Will" is familiar to many. Concern for Dying is an educational council in New York City which offers the Living Will forms at no charge (although a contribution of any amount is appreciated and is tax deductible). The one-page document is intended for your family, physician, lawyer, and all others whom your death may concern. It declares:

> Death is as much a reality as birth, growth, maturity and old age—it is the one certainty of life. If the time comes when I can.no longer take part in decisions for my own future, let this statement stand as an expression of my wishes and direction, while I am still of sound mind.
>
> If at such time the situation should arise in which there is no reasonable expectation of my recovery from extreme physical or mental disability, I direct that I be allowed to die and not be kept alive by medications, artificial means or "heroic measures." I do, however, ask that medication be mercifully administered to me to alleviate suffering even though this may shorten my remaining life.
>
> This statement is made after careful consideration and is in accordance with my strong convictions and beliefs. I want the wishes and directions here expressed carried out to the extent permitted by law. Insofar as they are not legally enforceable, I hope that those to whom this will is addressed will regard themselves as morally bound by these provisions.

The form allows for optional specific provisions to be inserted. It also has an optional Durable Power of Attorney section in which you designate someone to serve as your attorney-in-fact for the purpose of making medical treatment decisions in the event that you become incompetent or otherwise unable to make such decisions for yourself.

Concern for Dying also has a Living Will Registry, a newsletter, and offers materials such as a bibliography, information on films, selected articles, and case histories, questions and answers about the Living Will, and a condensed version of the Living Will which can be carried in a wallet in case of accident or emergency.

For more information about the organizations in this chapter, contact:

Clear Light Society
P. O. Box 306
Brookline, MA 02146
(617) 734-2939

Concern for Dying
250 West 57th Street
Room 831
New York, NY 10107
(212) 246-6962

Hanuman Foundation
   Dying Project
P. O. Box 2228
Taos, NM 87571

Hanuman Foundation
   Tape Library
P. O. Box 2320
Delray Beach, FL 33447

Hemlock Society
P. O. Box 66218
Los Angeles, CA 90066
(213) 391-1871 and
(213) 390-0470

Hospice Institute for
 Education, Training and
 Research
61 Burban Drive
Branford, CT 06405
(203) 481-6231

National Hospice
 Organization
1901 North Fort Myer Drive
#307
Arlington, VA 22209
(703) 243-5900

Elisabeth Kübler-Ross
 Center
South Route 616
Head Waters, VA 24442
(703) 396-3441

Shanti Project
525 Howard Street
San Francisco, CA 94105
(415) 777-3273

15
Out-of-Body Experience—
The Ecstasy of
Astral Projection

Ekstasy is the ancient Greek word from which the English "ecstasy" comes. Ordinarily we understand ecstasy to mean some delightful emotional state—rapture, perhaps, or swooning. It means "to stand outside of," to be outside of your normal everyday sense of self. In its original meaning, however, it denoted out-of-body experience (OBE). *Ex*, out of, and *stasis*, a fixed or static condition, is the ancient way of describing "the flight of the soul" or astral projection—the experience in which you find your consciousness or your center of self-awareness floating in space exterior to your physical body. In the OBE condition, you are fully and normally conscious. That is, you know you are not dreaming or fantasizing. Also, you perceive some portion of your environment which could not possibly be perceived from where your physical body is at that time. You are truly, literally, "outside yourself."

The effect of having an OBE, parapsychologist Dr. Charles Tart tells us, is enormous. In almost all cases, the person's reaction is approximately, "I no longer *believe* in survival after death—I *know* my consciousness will survive death because I have *experienced* my consciousness existing outside my physical body." The conviction gained by OBE experiencers that they will survive death, Tart adds, has undoubtedly led to the concept of soul.

Therefore the OBE, I myself add, has significance in major religious and spiritual traditions, although it is largely unrecognized as such by contemporary religionists, including priests and theologians.

Tart's statement can be found in his chapter on out-of-body experience in *Psychic Exploration*. Another contributor to that book, parapsychologist D. Scott Rogo, who is himself an experienced OBE "flier," has recently said that his research shows that many people who have the out-of-body experience later look back upon it as a "rehearsal for death" and, as such, regard it as proving the immortality of the personality. Listen to some of the comments Rogo gathered from OBE cases, as reported in his book on the surviving of death, *The Welcoming Silence*:

> The knowledge I gained at that time assured me of a future life.

> It makes me feel certain that there is a life after death which does not require a material body for us to be able to see and hear, and that we shall retain our personality.

> Death is like passing from twilight into the glories of the full midday sunshine.

> I know that death does not end all.

> I was always afraid to die, but not now.

> To me there is nothing truer than 'there is no death.'

Just as reincarnation studies are proving that time is no limitation to the survival of human personality, OBE research is demonstrating that space is no limitation either. Consciousness transcends time and space. In fact, from the point of view of those who best understand the nature of consciousness—mystics and spiritual teachers—time and space are illusions *derived* from consciousness; specifically, from the ordinary state of consciousness which also creates the illusion of ego. This is precisely the message of the great religious traditions: we are infinite and eternal. Cosmic consciousness shows this through direct experience to be perfectly true. Later in this chapter I will discuss whether and how you yourself might experience the out-of-body condition. First, however, I want to present a bit more information about the condition itself. There are many good books on the subject: Herbert Greenhouse's *The Astral Journey*, David Black's *Ekstasy*, Robert Crookall's *The Study and Practice of Astral Projection*, Sylvan Muldoon's *Projection of the Astral Body*, and Oliver Fox's *Astral Projection*. These all have interesting case histories, such as the following which Rogo reports in *The Welcoming Silence:*

> This case, a rather old one, occurred in 1863. Mrs. Wilmot, at home in Bridgeport, Connecticut, was in severe anxiety over her husband, who was making a trans-Atlantic voyage on the *City of Limerick* during stormy and dangerous weather. Upon going to sleep, she had the experience of leaving her body at rest in order to seek him. She saw herself crossing the sea, finding a black steamship, and seeking out her husband's room. She noted that the stateroom her husband was occupying with another man had an upper berth which extended back farther than the lower one. She saw the other man but nevertheless bent down and kissed her husband.
>
> Simultaneous to this experience by his wife, Wilmot himself had a dream of seeing his wife enter the room and kiss him. His statement reads, "Toward morning I dreamed that I saw my wife, whom I had left in the United States, come to the door of my stateroom, clad in her night dress. At the door she seemed to discover that I was not the only occupant of the room, hesitated a little, then advanced to my side, stooped down and kissed me, and after gently caressing me for a few moments, quietly withdrew."
>
> Upon awakening, Wilmot's cabinmate, William Tait, joked with him about having a woman enter his room at night!

The Wilmot case may seem remote, but similar events happen today also. The *National Enquirer* carries such stories almost every week! Here is an OBE account that appeared in the London *Sunday Times* of March 25, 1962, as a letter from a reader:

> During the war in the Western Desert, I was knocked unconscious by bomb blast and had the peculiar sensation of being out of my body viewing the scene from a point

about 20 feet above the ground. . . . I could hear the aircraft as it came in on another attack and the voices of my companions. I could see the dust clearing away from the explosion that had knocked me unconscious and my own body lying there on the gravel. . . .

I remember the thought, "I've got to get back," and then . . . I was back in my body consciously trying to force my eyes open. An odd thing was that, although I could hear perfectly while I was unconscious and could tell my comrades what they had said during that period, when I recovered consciousness I was stone deaf and remained so for two weeks afterwards. . . .

This experience has convinced me that there is a part of the person that survives death. . . . I am certain that when I do eventually die, or rather when my body dies, part of me will carry on, to where or to what I do not know.

OBEs have been recorded in every time and culture. Recent studies show that as many as 30% of the American population may have had them at least once. According to parapsychologist Dr. Stanley Krippner, three independent studies show that at least 3 out of 10 people have had OBEs.

These OBE reports have marked similarity to the experiences of people who are otherwise extremely different in terms of cultural background. Reports by Kansas housewives closely resemble OBE accounts from ancient Egyptian or oriental sources. St. Paul acknowledged the existence of the astral body in I Corinthians 15:40-44 (RSV); "There are celestial bodies and there are terrestrial bodies. . . . So it is with the resurrection of the dead. What is sown is perishable, what is raised is imperishable. . . . It is sown a physical body, it is raised a spiritual body."

St. Paul was speaking from personal experience. In II Corinthians 12:2 (RSV) he spoke of himself in the third person: "I know a man in Christ who fourteen years ago was caught up to the third heaven—whether in the body or out of the body I do not know, God knows. And I know that this man was caught up into Paradise—whether in the body or out of the body I do not know, God knows—and he heard things that cannot be told, which man may not utter."

Speaking on the same theme—initiation into cosmic mysteries—a friend who has explored occult traditions once told me that, according to the mystic scientist Rudolf Steiner, astral projection was part of the first initiation which students underwent in the ancient mystery schools centered around the Great Pyramid. From the King's Chamber they were taken in their astral bodies to the vicinity of the moon, where celestial beings of a more evolved nature than we humans—minor gods, if you will—instructed the students in still-greater mysteries. The students then returned to Earth and continued their esoteric studies and practices, having experienced directly their existence beyond the body. This is true rapture or swooning—not *losing* consciousness but *loosing* consciousness from its ego-bound state.

Along the same line, it may be of interest to know that according to esoteric Christianity, the true purpose of baptism is to induce an OBE and, thereby, demonstrate to the convert or initiate the reality of life after death. Baptism requires, from the esoteric point of view, that the person be held under water to the point of nearly drowning. This near-death experience, with an out-of-body experience likely to be included as part of it, initiates the person into the psychic mysteries "whereof it is unlawful to speak." Likewise, author-explorer Peter Freuchen reports that in Eskimo religious ceremonies an initiate would be virtually choked to death, i.e., until he passed out. It is probably more accurate to say "passed out of his body."

If all this seems fantastic or ridiculous to you, perhaps some solid scientific research literature will prove more acceptable. I summarized, in Chapter 2, Dr. Kenneth Ring's *Life at Death*, which shows that OBEs are frequently experienced by people in near-death situations. In another study of people who nearly died, Dr. Michael Sabom of the University of Florida, and a colleague, Sarah Kreutziger, found almost identical results. Their report appeared in *Theta* magazine in 1978.

Sabom and Kreutziger conducted a 20 month investigation, beginning in 1976, which studied 100 near-death

cases. They found that 16 patients who had been unconscious nevertheless viewed their own bodies and
physical surroundings from a detached position several
feet above ground. (Sabom and Kreutziger use the psychiatric term "autoscopy," meaning "to view oneself as if
outside the body," to describe the OBE condition.) Another
31 experienced "the passage of consciousness into a foreign
region or dimension." The report says:

> During the autoscopic experience, all patients noted a
> "floating" sensation "out of the body" unlike any felt
> before. While "detached" from the physical body, the
> patient observed his or her own body in clear detail. Nearby
> objects (many out of "view" of the patient's body) could
> often be seen (cardiac monitor behind the patient's bed,
> etc.). In most patients, observation of the type and sequence
> of resuscitation measures occurred at the time physiologic
> unconsciousness was most certain (during a grand mal
> seizure, cardioversion of ventricular fibrillation, injection
> of intracardiac medications, etc.). In one patient's words,
> "It was like sitting up in a balcony looking down at a movie."
> An overwhelming sense of calm and peace pervaded the
> whole episode. The experience ended abruptly and was
> followed by the regaining of consciousness.

The best collection of scientific reports on OBE research is, I feel, D. Scott Rogo's 1978 book, *Mind Beyond
the Body*. The fifteen articles, plus Rogo's useful commentaries, give a solid review of the best studies made on
the subject of out-of-body projection.

What has been found, in addition to the laboratory
evidence indicating that something does physically
separate from the material body, are characteristics of how
the OBE condition occurs and what it means. Generally
speaking, an OBE is a once-in-a-lifetime experience, although some people cultivate the ability and apparently
can leave their bodies at will. We'll consider this in a
moment. For most OBE experiencers, however, it comes
about as a result of grave illness, extreme emotional stress
or often it simply happens during sleep. Tart estimates in
his introduction to Robert Monroe's *Journeys Out of the*

Body that 90-95% of the people who have this experience are very glad, even joyful, it occurred, while 5% are frightened by it because they interpret what happens as meaning either that they are dying or are going crazy. Actually, neither of these fear-oriented interpretations is correct, but it's understandable that when you've never experienced an OBE before or even heard of it, the OBE can seem like death or insanity.

The most acceptable and enduring interpretation of the out-of-body experience is the religious one, as a liberation into a wider world—the world to which the soul goes after death and which the living can visit through dreams, meditation and psychic abilities such as astral projection.* However, these traditions also stress that cultivating psychic abilities can also be a spiritual dead end. St. Paul pointed out strongly in I Corinthians 12 that the "diversities of gifts" such as clairvoyance, prophecy, healing, medium-ship and so forth are "as sounding brass or a tinkling cymbal" without love as the essential element in your behavior. *The Tibetan Book of the Dead* also, in referring to the astral body separating from the physical body, indicates that attaining such a psychic power is far short of enlightenment or entering the Clear Light of the compassionate Buddha. In Garfield's meditation research, he found that the Tibetan Buddhist meditators he tested were reluctant to discuss OBE, even though they reported it during the interviews. One said, "I was not limited by my

---

*Psychoactive drugs have also been used by some occult and esoteric traditions as a means of inducing out-of-body experience. I will not consider them here, except to note that there is a *sub rosa* practice among a small group of scientific researchers and death education counselors to use a legal anesthetic, ketamine hydrochloride, for inducing OBE. Their purpose is psychotherapeutic; they use it to facilitate attitudinal change with regard to fear of dying. "It's the most effective thing I've seen," one doctor told me. "I'm using it with cancer patients and with people who have difficulty in letting go." He acknowledges that the practice, although not specifically illegal, may be considered improper by medical colleagues.

physical body. I could see my body sitting in the lotus position, meditating, but my consciousness could move around the room." Nevertheless, Garfield noted in his *Journal of Transpersonal Psychology* article, the Tibetan Buddhist meditators felt that displaying such psychic powers was "an impediment to ultimate enlightenment."

I offer these comments as a note of caution before discussing how you might undertake study of out-of-body projection. There is another thing to consider also: the lack of safeguards and ethical standards in the field of psychic development because no testing and licensing procedures exist. Generally speaking, I feel that people should be firmly "in" their bodies before trying to get "out." That is, psychic experiences can be overwhelming to someone lacking psychological stability and integration. Moreover, there are charlatans and hustlers galore who claim to offer experiences which seem alluring but which may, for the unwary, be more costly in money and personal comfort than they bargained for.

Perhaps the best-known course of instruction for teaching you how to project out of your body is the M-5000 course developed by Virginia businessman, Robert Monroe, whose OBE experiences are recounted in *Journeys Out of the Body*. I first met Monroe in 1973, some fifteen years after he began traveling in what he calls the "second body" but before he set up a school, the Monroe Institute of Applied Science, in Faber, Virginia, for teaching people astral travel. When we got together again four years later, as speakers at a conference, I was pleased to hear that things were progressing successfully. Elisabeth Kübler-Ross attended one of Monroe's courses, and speaks highly of it. The name of her center, Shanti Nilaya, was "given" to her during an OBE at Monroe's school.

An interview that Monroe gave to a reporter has some useful information for us, so I'll quote it here with his permission.

What happens to the body while you're out of it?
It's in a form of sleep, running on the automatic nervous system. Depending on the degree of the out-of-the-body

state, the body is either breathing heavily or in a near comatose condition. . . .

What exactly is the purpose of your M-5000 course?
It's an experimental program. We're running through some 5000 people to develop and evaluate a training system in order to understand, control and then utilize the basic bioenergy used to achieve the OBE. This energy comes in the form of a second body, that is, an intermediate mechanism by which the soul controls the physical body.

Why do we need another body to explain the OBE?
Once one stayed permanently from the physical body, that mechanism would more or less dissolve into the energy that you might label soul.

The idea of a second body is very common throughout history. Saints are often seen in their second bodies during apparitions. Ghosts are another example. The second body acts as a transformer of energy from the soul to the body. Frankly, I don't know why they exist.

Does every human being have the capacity for an OBE?
No question about it. Virtually everyone moves into an OBE during sleep; they just don't remember it.

What percentage of your experimenters actually undergo an OBE?
About 15 percent. Like many other things, this requires a great deal of practice. We do have, on the other hand, a 100 percent success factor in those that continue the exercises they have learned. But it may take several years [or it] may take several weeks.

How do you train people to have an OBE?
First of all, we teach people to put their physical bodies asleep while leaving the mind totally awake. Once the body is asleep and not interfering with the mind's activities, we instruct them how to actively utilize that mind. From then on, it's a matter of practice. . . .

Does the OBE imply immortality?
That's probably one of the principal reasons we're developing simplified training systems for the OBE. Moving the second body in the OBE is the most effective way to demonstrate the [unreality] of death. One can temporarily visit the energy system where you go after

you die. We teach terminal cases how to go to establish a beachhead in this other dimension and then they lose their fear of death.

How do you know that this is what occurs after death? Do you meet the spirits of dead people?
You can if you want. It happens. . . .

Monroe offers courses around the country, in addition to those at the Institute. For more information, write to: Monroe Institute of Applied Sciences, P.O. Box 175, Faber, VA 22938, (804) 361-1252. In addition, *Journeys Out of the Body* has two chapters describing Monroe's early techniques in simple step-by-step fashion.

Another course of instruction in OBE is offered by a spiritual system called Eckankar or just plain Eck. Founded in the 1960s by Paul Twitchell, Eckankar claims to be an ancient and direct "path to God" and a "path of total awareness." Eckists refer to OBE as "soul travel" and say they go far, far beyond the astral plane up to the highest plane the human soul can reach—God consciousness. You can learn more about Eckankar by reading Twitchell's book, *Eckankar: The Key to Secret Worlds*, which contains a chapter describing the Eck techniques of soul travel. You can also write for information to Eck headquarters: Eckankar, P.O. Box 3100, Menlo Park, CA 94025.

There are many other books that claim to teach the techniques of astral projection. You can find them advertised in magazines such as *Fate, New Realities,* and others in the psychic/occult field. Another word of caution, however. Rogo's comprehensive survey of the methods given in books led him to state in *The Welcoming Silence:* ". . . although these techniques may work for the Foxes, Muldoons, and Monroes, there is scarcely any evidence that they would work for anyone else."

In addition to books, you can find cassette tape courses of instruction. The American Research Team at 256 South Robertson Blvd., Beverly Hills, CA 90211 offers an interesting tape of "astral sounds" that they claim have triggered out-of-body experiences in people who have tried many other methods but failed. So does Pyramid Books, 214 Derby Street, Salem, MA 01970. My own experiments with taped methods were not successful in inducing an OBE, but they were interesting and relaxing experiences nevertheless. I make no claim for these tapes; I simply offer the information. In all cases—from paying for instruction to actually getting out of the body—beware. Or to put it in positive terms: from buying to flying, be aware!

16
You Have Died Before—
Reincarnation and
Past Life Therapy

Have you lived before? If so, then you have died before. The theory of reincarnation says this is precisely the case. You have lived and died many times as an evolving soul moving through time, through history, to a fuller and larger existence, and ultimately a total reunion with the All. In Chapter 2, I said that reincarnation was not proven definitively, but there is a great deal of evidence suggesting its reality—evidence which cannot be explained away by any other interpretation. Psychic researchers conclude that it would be absurd to dismiss it all as simply involving coincidence because the agreement of facts is too consistent and too complex. The best-known reincarnation researcher, Dr. Ian Stevenson, has published several books describing the best cases of thousands he has collected.

Lately some psychologists and counselors have been using hypnosis to regress people to what the people themselves feel are prior lives. The purpose of this "past life therapy" is to help the person deal with problems in his present life which apparently are due to conditions that have carried over from a past life—or even several lifetimes! For example, a recent article in the *National Star* newspaper reported how Ralph Grossi, a hypnotist in Pittsburgh who holds group sessions in West Virginia,

Pennsylvania, and Ohio, cured headaches, crippling illnesses, backaches and emotional problems by taking people back into former lives where their current problems started. Grossi claims that by re-entering a former life through hypnosis, patients can find the origin of the problem and stop it from torturing them in this life. One patient, a 30-year-old woman, went to Grossi to lose weight, and found that she also lost the throbbing migraine headaches that had plagued her throughout her life. Mrs. Georgie Riser of Martin's Ferry, Ohio, told the *Star*, "I had migraine headaches ever since I could remember. Doctors always treated it as a sinus problem. They drained my sinuses, treated me with nerve medicine, gave me shots, but nothing helped."

Then Grossi regressed Mrs. Riser to her previous life as a bar girl in a Wild West saloon in the late 1800s. "I was a saloon hall girl named Jessica Andrews," said Mrs. Riser, "and I had a boy friend who fought with General Custer and was killed at the Battle of Little Big Horn. A fight broke out in the bar and guns were fired. One shot hit Jessie in the head. She was killed." That episode, the *Star* reported, made Mrs. Riser realize that her migraine headaches stemmed from a past life. She had been subconsciously holding onto memories from that life, according to Grossi. "I haven't had a headache since I went to Grossi, about three years ago," Mrs. Riser remarked.

Skeptics may object that this experience hardly constitutes scientific research since there were no records kept, no controls or structured experiment, etc. Moreover, it could be that Mrs. Riser's headaches were cured by placebo effect—expectation and strong belief—and had nothing to do with remembering a prior life, let alone living one. I would agree with those objections to this case. In fact, I would also point out that Ian Stevenson himself has stated that hypnosis is useless as a tool for reincarnation research except in cases where past life memories have *spontaneously* arisen. In those cases hypnosis can be useful, he says. But if you take a person who has no notion of having lived prior to this life, and tell him he is going to remember his previous incarnation, all you can be sure of finding is creative imagination. The behavior of people under hypnosis is understood well enough to know that they will try hard to please the hypnotist, acting on the slightest suggestion or subtlest cue creating all sorts of fantastic stories which *they themselves then sincerely believe*. Whether or not the person lived previous to this life, he will produce all sorts of "data" indicating that he did. "Jessica Andrews" might be such a fictional production.

As with the other areas of research indicating post-mortem survival, we walk a fine line here between having an open mind and having a hole in the head. Therefore, we can be thankful for the credible work of researchers with good credentials who have begun to study the possibility of reincarnation in a rigorous way. Not only have they gathered strong indications of past life memories from thousands of people, they have also discovered something which is of major significance for our purposes here: *past life recall can alleviate fear of dying*.

One of the most notable people in this field is a psychologist, Dr. Helen Wambach, author of several books on the subject of reincarnation memories. Her first was *Reliving Past Lives: The Evidence Under Hypnosis*. A review of it in *Brain/Mind Bulletin* by editor Marilyn Ferguson noted that Wambach "has devised an elegant scientific methodology for studying the possible validity of 'memories' of previous lifetimes. Her evidence is so professionally marshalled that one must conclude that her subject merits further exploration." Wambach drew her data from more than 1,000 "past-life recalls" by hypnotized subjects. They provided information about their culture, technology, environment and personal history. These "memories" coalesced into demographic, economic and cultural patterns that mirrored historic and statistical data with remarkable accuracy. Collusion among the subjects was ruled out.

The hypnotic sessions were conducted in small groups and lasted all day. Wambach recorded data in detail, noting

observations of costume, money, skin color, clothing, foot-
wear, foods, architecture and eating utensils. The cumula-
tive data showed a breakdown of social class appropriate
for the historic eras. The vast majority of her subjects
(60-77% in all the time periods) reported themselves to
have led humble lives as slaves, peasants, soldiers, and
merchants. Relatively few were middle-class, fewer still
were upper-class, and only one claimed to have been an
important historical figure (President James Buchanan).
Wambach reported:

> The great majority of my subjects went through their lives
> wearing rough homespun garments, living in crude huts,
> eating bland cereal grain with their fingers from wooden
> bowls. Some of these lives were spent as primitive food-
> gatherers or nomadic hunters. But the majority of lower-
> class lives in all periods belonged to people who farmed
> the land in whatever part of the world they found them-
> selves. . . . If they were fantasizing these past lives, why
> would they choose such drudgery to recall?

Wambach's subjects would frequently report things
that puzzled them and Wambach herself, but they nevertheless turned out to be accurate for the time and place.
For instance, five data sheets described lives in the 2000-
1000 B.C. era in a region around the Caucasus in what is
now Russia. The hypnotized people described the area as
mountainous and barren. When asked to visualize a map
representing the area, they saw it as north of Iran toward
Pakistan. All five said that they had been surprised to find
themselves fairskinned in that part of the world. Three
described their hair as light brown, two as blond. (The
original Caucasians were fair.) Also, all five saw themselves as wearing a kind of leather pants, but trousers were
highly unusual in regressions to these early periods. In the
period 2000-1000 B.C., "only in this region did my subjects
see themselves wearing pants," Wambach wrote. Costume
research eventually showed that the Scythians and
Parthians, early descendents of the Caucasians, wore
leather trousers.

It was this sort of "wrong"-information-that-turned-out-to-be-right that gave strongest indication the data were related to something real. More to the point of this book, however, the subjects' reports of their reactions to dying were surprisingly consistent. Most reported either calm, peaceful acceptance (49%) or even joy and release (30%). Fear or sorrow (10%) were usually associated with a violent death or the death of a mother leaving young children behind. Many of the subjects said that hypnotic regression had freed them of their fear of death.

Wambach's second book, *Life Before Life*, contains many interesting case histories from her research. It is based on an article which she published in 1977 in a magazine *Psychic* (now retitled *New Realities*). I had a lengthy discussion with her on her research shortly after her article appeared, and again during the course of writing this book. Chapter 3 of *Life Before Life* has further insights into the usefulness of past life recall, or, more specifically, past death recall. Wambach writes:

> Admittedly, it's one thing to "fantasize" or "remember" past deaths and another thing to actually experience death. I made no claims that experiencing "past life recall" in my hypnotic workshops was therapeutic in any way. Yet many subjects told me that they had lost their fear of death after the workshop experience.
>
> "You know, I felt I was making up my past lives in your workshop. Didn't think it was real. But a couple of days later, I realized that something had happened; something important to me," Nancy told me. We'd met at a friend's house a month after Nancy had been in my workshop. "I used to be terrified of going under anesthesia, even for pulling a tooth. I fought the idea of being unconscious. I thought it was like death and I was plain scared. But after 'imagining' my death in a past life, I'm not afraid of death, or of being unconscious."
>
> So I knew that 90 percent of my subjects found that death was pleasant. Yet none of them reported that they had lost their zest for life.

When I spoke with Wambach recently, she volunteered an additional insight that isn't in her books. It seems from her research that present life phobias, when due to an experience in a previous life or lives, are not the result simply of having had a traumatic experience in the previous life but rather of *not having resolved or integrated the trauma in that life.* "If people die with a lot of fear, confusion and resentment," she told me, "*that* is what causes a phobia in a later life." She illustrated her point with the case of a woman who feared to go swimming. Through hypnotic regression, this phobia was traced to incidents in two previous lives in which she had drowned. Granted that those are traumatic experiences, it nevertheless seems from Wambach's research that even if the woman had not actually drowned in those lifetimes, her present life phobia could still have resulted because the fright of near-drowning had been so great in each past life and it had never been relieved or resolved.

This points up all the more strongly your own need to face the fear of dying and conquer it. Reincarnation research indicates that *you'll be back*, and what you don't deal with in this life you'll have to face in another. It's best to do it here and now, sages and saints tell us. Get off the wheel of death and rebirth in *this* lifetime.

What resources are available to you if you wish to pursue past life recall? Books, tapes, and courses are advertised in national magazines such as *New Realities, Fate, New Age, East West Journal, Venture Inward, Body Mind Spirit* and *Psychology Today.* I can recommend the paperback *You Will Live Again* by Brad Steiger. Dick Sutphen has developed a past life hypnotic regression course which is available on tape from: Valley of the Sun Publishing, P.O. Box 38, Malibu, CA 90265.

Wambach offers a training seminar for professional researchers, who then are qualified to use her group hypnotic technique and offer seminars to the public. If you'd like to be referred to a Wambach-trained researcher, write for information to: Dr. Helen Wambach, P.O. Box 581, Concord, CA 94520.

Remember, however, that playing ego games with past life recall is *not* the point. I've seen some people trot out their alleged previous incarnations as if they were trophies, and then indulge in the most unbecoming verbal behavior, glorifying themselves and bragging to impress others. Such "memories," no matter how real they may be from the historian's point of view, are doing the person no good whatsoever. They are at best amusing and frivolous. And even if the person has documented the historical validity of his previous lives, demonstrating that he didn't get the information through normal but subconscious means (cryptoamnesia), it still doesn't serve the purpose we are concerned with here. The point of your exploration is therapeutic—to reduce your fear of dying by understanding yourself, your *true* self, better. That self may take on many physical bodies over the course of time, but it transcends them all. Learn who you *really* are, and get off the wheel of reincarnation.

17
A Closer Look at Heaven and Hell

A young samurai warrior stood respectfully before an aged Zen master and said, "Master, teach me about heaven and hell." The master snapped up his head in disgust and said, "Teach you about heaven and hell? Why, I doubt that you could even learn to keep your sword from rusting! You ignorant fool! How dare you suppose that you could understand anything I might have to say?"

The old man went on and on, becoming even more insulting, while the young swordman's surprise turned first to confusion and then to hot anger, rising by the minute. Master or no master, who can insult a samurai and live?

At last, with teeth clenched and blood nearly boiling in fury, the warrior blindly drew his sword and prepared to end the old man's sharp tongue and life all in a moment. The master looked straight into his eyes and said gently, "That's hell."

At the peak of his rage, the samurai realized that this was indeed his teaching. The master had hounded him into a living hell, driven by uncontrolled anger and ego. The young man, profoundly humbled, sheathed his sword and bowed low to this great spiritual teacher. Looking up into the wise man's aged, beaming face, he felt more love and compassion than he had ever felt in his life, at which point the master raised his index finger as would a schoolteacher and said, "And that's heaven."

Is it practical to discuss heaven and hell? My answer is: Yes, if the discussion gives you new insight and offers a basis for ridding yourself of superstition and fear. That is what I propose to do here.

Heaven and hell are popularly thought of as *places* in the universe, locations in space where the spirits of the dead go. To quote evangelist Billy Graham: "I believe the Bible teaches that heaven is a literal place." To a degree, this is correct. The evidence from out-of-body and near-death cases indicates a journey of the soul beyond this three-dimensional physical world into other sets of dimensions. However, as I will show in the final chapter, there is a journey only insofar as there is a *separate self*, an ego of some sort, which thinks it has someplace to go.

Is there intelligence in the universe higher than human? Microbes go their microbial way with a lifespan measured in days, presumably unaware of, say, insects, which can be seen as an example of the next higher level. And just as insects surpass microbes in intelligence, longevity, size, and organic complexity, so do humans surpass insects.

Microbes, insects, and people co-exist, but rarely are they aware of the others' activities and domains. How often do we intrude into the life of a gnat, an ant, or a termite? Logically speaking, however, if life exists at the microbial, insect, and human levels, why should it end there? It has been evolving on earth for several billion years. But the sun is a relatively young star. There are many others in the universe far older than our home star whose planetary systems could have life-favorable conditions for much longer than here on Earth. Life on those planets could have evolved far beyond the human level in terms of intelligence, longevity, size, and organic complexity to the point where we humans might be a mere gnat to them—or smaller!

So, theoretically speaking, there could be higher forms of life in the universe. Of course, we'd ordinarily presume them to be in a physical, three-dimensional form such as we are, with technology and a need to eat, drink, sleep and perform biological functions. That is the picture we get from exobiologists, who search for life in the universe.

Dr. Carl Sagan, astronomer-author of *Other Worlds*, recently wrote: "It is roughly estimated that there are more than one million technical civilizations in our Milky Way galaxy alone that are more advanced than ours."

But must life assume the conditions with which we are familiar? Speaking theoretically again, there's no reason it should. The diversity of forms with which we're already familiar—land- and sea-living plants and animals ranging from viruses and algae to whales and redwoods—has recently been expanded by the discovery of plasmatic creatures whose native habitat is the upper atmosphere. As claimed by Trevor James Constable in *Sky Creatures— Living UFOs* (Pocket Books, 1978), these biological aero- forms are normally invisible because they inhabit the infrared portion of the electromagnetic spectrum. They are not solid, liquid, or gaseous, but plasma—the fourth state of matter. (Fire is a common example of plasma.) Occasionally they change their density and emerge into the visible portion of the spectrum, at which time they may be seen by humans as a pulsating red-to-orange glow in the sky. These strange aerial organisms, which Constable dubbed "critters," appear to be, he says,

> . . . an elemental branch of evolution probably older than most life on earth, dating from the time when the planet was more gaseous and plasmatic than solid. They are part of what occultists term "elementals." They live invisibly like fish in the ocean of atmosphere. Like fish, I estimate them to be of low intelligence. They will probably one day be better classified as belonging to the general field of macrobiology or even macrobacteria inhabiting the aerial ocean we call the sky.

In *Sky Creatures*, Constable offers photographs of critters, along with evidence obtained from other sources that support his claim. He also offers simple instructions by which anyone can take pictures of critters. In my judgment, Constable has greatly expanded our scientific knowledge of reality.

Now, this is an important point in considering whether heaven and hell are also real. If plasmatic animals have been living invisibly in the atmosphere for eons, but we have only recently become aware of them in objective scientific terms, what else might there be in reality which ancient traditions have asserted but science has overlooked or denied?

Many people reject the notion of heaven and hell because, they feel, it is "unscientific." But is it? That depends on how you define science. Many scientists presume that the material world is all there is to reality because that is all they can observe. Their philosophy of existence is called scientific materialism, and they wrongly equate that with science itself. Now, if you define the universe solely in terms of sensory data, naturally you're not going to believe that extrasensory perceptions are possible. You're going to say that extrasensory is non-sensory—i.e., nonsense.

Since the afterlife worlds are imperceptible to the normal physical senses, they are beyond the range of present scientific observation. However, they may not always be. Just as the photographs of critters take us into the borderland of physical reality, there are researchers apparently close to demonstrating in objective scientific terms that electronic communication with the dead is possible. This kind of breakthrough should make quite clear to people that there is a fundamental difference between the *method* of science used by all scientists and the *philosophy* of science held by most scientists. The method of science provides data; the philosophy of science interprets that data. All too often the data of the scientific method are ignored, distorted, or misinterpreted by materialistic scientists, whose basic assumptions—their philosophy of science—operate unconsciously to screen out what doesn't agree with their conception of reality.

Do you see my point? If heaven and hell are first of all conceived of naively as mere places or locations in familiar space, then when the most powerful telescopes don't reveal them, it seems to be proof that they're not real. And if you have a basic idea about reality being limited to observations by the physical senses, then when someone claims to have made extrasensory observations, you dismiss them as nonsense because they do not conform to your idea of what's real and unreal, possible and impossible, in the universe. Consequently, from the perspective of scientific materialism, heaven and hell are simply childish fantasies. But from the perspective of someone who has enlarged his scale of observation beyond the sensory to the extrasensory, reality as scientific materialism defines it is itself a fantasy based upon a constricted and partial awareness that filters out as much, if not more, than it lets in.

Our sense of reality, then, is a function of our state of consciousness. This is an extremely important point to grasp. Reality itself is unchanging, but our sense of reality—our understanding of how the universe is structured and operates—is dependent upon our state of awareness. Our worldview depends upon how fully we perceive and experience our existence. Culture tends to create obstacles and screens in the mind which prevent people from seeing clearly just *what is*. But nature has a way of getting around our social conditioning and waking us up. It has a way of kicking out the cultural underpinnings of our conventional ideas about reality. Various life experiences, such as extreme illness, stress, accident, or loss of a loved one, can propel people right through their tight little notions into a more direct perception of their existence. They see how fragile their lives are, how shallow their values are, how fleeting their pleasures and treasures, how truly vast the universe is.

Psychic experiences also give a larger view of reality. Moreover, parapsychology demonstrates that the scientific method is quite capable of revealing and investigating those nonphysical realms in which psychic phenomena occur. Parapsychologists have a larger range of observation than strictly materialistic scientists, although their method of observation is the same. Thus, despite resistance by dogmatic scientists, the scientific case for other worlds grows stronger daily. That's not to say that science will prove heaven and hell exist, as you'll see in a moment. It *is* to say, however, that the logic of science and the power of empiric observation are helping nature to demolish the conceptual barriers in our own minds—barriers which prevent clear perception of the other worlds in reality.

One of the most dramatic modern accounts of other worlds is *Return from Tomorrow*, the story of Dr. George Ritchie, a Virginia psychiatrist, who nearly died in an Army hospital. His near-death experience is a fascinating report of his insights into some realms of the post-mortem condition during the time he was clinically dead. When he and I appeared together on "The Beverly Sills Show" a few years ago, along with author-parapsychologist Martin Ebon, Ritchie—a devout Christian—gave a brief summary of his experiences. Afterward I remarked that this story, which inspired Moody's research into near-death cases, illustrated St. Peter's admonition to add knowledge to one's faith.

It was another apostle, St. Paul, who pointed out that the proper term is heavens—plural—not heaven. In other words, embracing and interpenetrating the three-dimensional world with which we are familiar, there are other worlds, other planes of existence, other realms of nature. As I said, science is now beginning to recognize the multidimensionality of the universe in which you can pass from one set of dimensions to another, as in the notion that black holes in space connect matter and antimatter universes.

The process by which apparently separate worlds coexist, or the process by which a soul or spirit passes from one world to another, is not understood by conventional science. But a very promising breakthrough has been made in the theoretical work of Thomas Bearden, whose book *The Excalibur Briefing* (Strawberry Hill Press, 1980) offers an exciting unified field theory to explain the physics of paranormal phenomena. Long before Bearden, however, occult and spiritual traditions maintained that they had such information. Moreover, they claimed to have detailed "maps" of the various realms of existence which constitute reality. My books *Future Science* and *Other Worlds, Other Universes* examine those maps.

The terminology used on the maps varies from tradition

to tradition, and as I noted in Chapter 2, there are cultural overlays that tend to obscure the situation. In the Judeo-Christian cosmology or account of the universe, these interpenetrating sets of dimensions are called the heavens. In Hinduism and Buddhism, they are called *lokas*. Some occult systems speak of levels or zones of consciousness. The terminology differs from culture to culture, and so does the imagery, but the underlying concept is the same.

One of the most useful contemporary presentations of the nature of the afterlife worlds is found in a book by Dr. George Meek, whom I mentioned in Chapter 2. In *After We Die, What Then?*° he offers what he calls "A Blueprint of Immortality," showing, in a large multi-colored diagram with accompanying text, what post-mortem existence is like.

Interpenetrating our world, he says, are the astral planes, the still-higher mental and causal planes, and finally the celestial planes. The lowest astral plane is traditionally referred to as hell, hades, or purgatory. The Bible describes it as "outer darkness, weeping, wailing and gnashing of teeth...." This "dark, dismal, dangerous and often frightening world," as Meek describes it, is populated with greedy, self-centered, unloving, resentful people. Often they have fierce bodily desires and lusts. They may be drug addicts, sex perverts, alcoholics, murderers, or suicides.

The intermediate and higher astral planes offer much more pleasant experiences for the dead—"wider perspectives, greater vistas, magnificent panoramas," Meek says. Help and love are offered to souls, along with further growth opportunities for advancement to the mental and causal planes. On these levels of consciousness, there is access to all of the accumulated wisdom of the ages.

On the celestial planes, there is preliminary conscious contact with the Universal Godhead. This is the level of consciousness from which the world's saviors, sages, and *avatars* enter human existence.

°Available from Metascience Foundation, P.O. Box 747, Franklin, NC 28734.

All these planes or levels are said by esoteric, occult and spiritual tradition to have beings native to them—angels, devas, herukas, elementals, demons, unclean spirits, cherubim, seraphim, archangels and all the other heavenly or hellish "mythological" creatures generally dismissed by materialists as fantastic nonsense. Some of these intelligences have been perceived by people during OBEs and near-death experiences as "beings of light." Their native condition on the causal and celestial planes normally keeps them invisible to us. Likewise on the lower planes, ghosts and apparitions are normally unseen. And on the lowest astral level, Meek tells us, creatures of non-human lines of evolution may attach themselves to the auras or astral bodies of people living on Earth. Such a "possessed" person may act abnormally, be judged insane and institutionalized, or commit suicide.

Because I've found Meek's "blueprint of immortality" to be so useful, I've drawn from it here and heartily recommend that you read the entire book, which is short and simply-written. I would like to quote for your benefit, however, this passage in which Meek discusses Jesus's teaching about the nature of his mission:

> Strange and unbelievable as it may seem, the Nazarene was telling the literal truth when he said, "The Kingdom of Heaven is *within* you!" He was not speaking in parables. The only problem is that during almost all of the past 2,000 years, man and his "sciences" have not known enough about the nature of his own existence and the so-called material world to be able to comprehend His teaching.

Heaven and hell, then, can be described as real places extending through the universe, but paradoxically, they are contacted right here on Earth within you. That is because heaven and hell are also psychological conditions, states of mind. As such, they are a function of your own state of consciousness, whether in the body or out of it. In other words, heaven and hell are hyperspaces, sets of dimensions that we experience as states of mind and that commingle with the familiar physical space-time framework we ordinarily call the cosmos. As psychological states, heaven and hell are indeed the conditions that prevail "between the ears," i.e., *within* your mind. But conventional psychology, which tends to consider "mind" as confined within the body, especially within the brain, must reckon with parapsychology and paraphysics. These disciplines show that there is an extrasomatic aspect to mind, that our psychological activity extends beyond the body.

Recently some psychologists have begun to speak quite metaphysically. They speak of a holographic universe in which instantaneous transfer of information is possible, i.e., ESP. They also speak of a "field of mind" surrounding the planet. This mind field or collective unconscious, of which we are all a part, is composed of psychic energy or thought energy, and contains the record of human experience throughout history. It can be imagined as an envelope or shell of mind energy extending into space, much like the atmosphere. And just as we all have lungs and breathe the same air, so do we all have brains and participate in the same mental environment. But depending on various factors—heredity, family, culture—we don't participate to the same degree, just as we don't all have the same lung capacity and freedom of breathing due to anatomical obstructions, physiological factors such as emphysema, and emotional factors such as those that give rise to asthma or a muscularly-constricted abdomen.

To put it simply: Heaven and hell are *both* places and states of mind. Insofar as they are places, they are dimensionalities interpenetrating our physical world. Insofar as they are states of mind, they are experienced within, psychologically. You are at the center of all worlds, here and now.

Is there anything that can account for this? Yes—consciousness. Consciousness is the meeting ground for inner and outer reality, for psychology and physics. In seeking to understand the nature of heaven and hell, inner space research and outer space research come together. All that we can know about "out there" is very much conditioned upon what is "in here." Our state of consciousness determines our understanding of reality. Those who know reality fully are those who first of all know themselves and have removed all impediments of mind and character that prevent clear perception. The knower and the known become one. Who are these people? And how might we become like them? Read on.

18

How Can You Die
Since You Were
Never Born?

To fear death, gentlemen, is nothing other than to think
oneself wise when one is not; for it is to think one knows
what one does not know. No man knows whether death
may not even turn out to be the greatest of blessings for
a human being and yet people fear it as if they knew
for certain that it is the greatest of evils.

Socrates, just before drinking
the hemlock poison.

Philosophy, said Plato in his *Phaedo*, is the practice or
rehearsal of death. He also declared, echoing his teacher
Socrates, that the unexamined life is not worth living. To
that I would add: nor is the unexamined death. I will explain.

I have tried to show throughout this book that whether
or not we are aware of it, we are all philosophers. That
is, we all have beliefs and assumptions—usually unrecognized ones—that amount to a philosophy of life and death,
and that influence our behavior and vitality. Therefore, I
have had you examine your philosophy and then deliberately go through rehearsals for your own death. I have
had you practice philosophy in the sense that Plato meant.
In this final chapter, I want to be philosophical in a formal
way. I want to address directly the question that has been
hovering over our rehearsals for death: Who or what dies?
I've touched on this question from time to time, but it is
now possible to examine it explicitly and in depth.

165

We have seen thus far that your personality survives death of the body and in all likelihood will reincarnate. But to what end? Death doesn't automatically make a saint of a sinner, or a sage of a fool. If your previous lives and deaths have taught you nothing, your future lives and deaths will be merely stupid repetitions of the sins and errors you've been committing, the follies and vices you've been pursuing. Your contribution to human happiness and wisdom will be a great big zero, and you'll be remembered —if at all—for your addition to the world's confusion and misery.

Death challenges us to find the meaning of life, and with it, genuine happiness. It is nature's way of goading us to discover our true condition, our real self—beyond the transience and ephemerality of this material world. And not only this world, but *all* worlds. Remember what I said in the first chapter: in this book you will find that death is your best friend. If your best friend challenges you, surely it must be well-intended for a single purpose—to make you happy and wise. That is the purpose of death. Let's see more specifically what this means.

In Frederick H. Holck's excellent anthology, *Death and Eastern Thought*, an essay by W.R. LaFleur quotes the Zen Master Hakuin on the use of a "death koan":

> If you should have the desire to study Zen under a teacher and see into your own nature, you should first investigate the word *shi* (death). If you want to know how to investigate this word, then at all times while walking, standing, sitting, or reclining, without despising activity, without being caught up in quietude, merely investigate the koan: "After you are dead and cremated, where has the main character gone?" Then in a night or two or at most a few days, you will obtain the decisive and ultimate great joy. Among all the teachings and instructions, the word *death* has the most unpleasant and disgusting connotations. Yet if you once suddenly penetrate this "death" koan, you will find that there is no more felicitous teaching than this instruction that serves as the key to the realm in which birth and death are transcended, where the place in which you stand is the Diamond indestructible, and where you have become a divine immortal, unaging and undying.

This condition is nirvana or the Kingdom of Heaven. It is the essential state, the Condition of all conditions—that which all enlightened teachers and spiritual traditions have as the heart of their mission and their efforts to communicate to people. The essence of you, the real you, is beyond birth and death. Stepping off the wheel of rebirth, those teachers and traditions tell us, is possible for anyone at any time by realizing his condition prior to that which he mistakenly thinks is his true identity. And what is that prior condition? To put it bluntly: *You are God.*

This is the core truth of all the world's major sacred traditions. The very essence of all creation—God—is as much within you as it is within trees, mountains, stars and cosmic dust. The condition from which all existence springs —God—is your true identity. When you fully realize the nature of your being, you recognize there is no separation from God and never has been. You are infinite and eternal. You are immortal—not as a separate body or soul in a single permanent state but as that which produces the totality of the universe in all states.

Enlightenment is simply waking up from the dream of conventional life generated by the ego-based sense of separate self. And in the enlightened state, all apparently separate forms of life and conditions of existence are seen to be masks of God—forms in which the divine source of all worlds and beings chooses to hide a part of Itself. Understanding this is what Jesus called "entering the Kingdom." Fundamentally speaking, then, hell is separation from God, heaven is union with God, and the crucial difference is one's state of consciousness.

Many people have said, "I am God" without realizing the least bit of what the words truly signify. Mental asylums are full of such folk. But so are honored institutions such as government, religion, science, business, the military— in fact, wherever and whenever anyone attempts to elevate himself to a position of power, fame, wealth, or status that seems to offer immortality for the ego-centered person. They may not have uttered the words aloud, but the thought is there nevertheless, moving them to seek the status of God and foolishly trying to apply that status to their physical, worldly condition.

Such cases of mistaken identity occur to some degree in everyone who does not recognize that his very self, his being (including life and death), is not only from God—it is God. What is there that is *not* God? Thus, to realize our true self in its perfect "formless form" is to realize God as All, as none other than the totality of existence, and that from which all being arises.

That is your real self, your true identity. But notice: "I am God" does not apply to your personality, your conventional ego. Neither does it mean you alone are God. Nor does it mean you are identical to some deity in the sky.

A genuine realization of God as your true self does not give you exclusive status, however talented, intelligent, charismatic, or otherwise special you may be. Such delusions of grandeur are what brought Jim Jones and his followers to the Guyana massacre. A genuine realization of God as your self is humbling. It dissolves the boundaries of thought and perception which led you to think of yourself as a separate body or a special personality or even a separate soul. Understand that the ego can create the illusion of separateness and identify it with a celestial body of ethereal substance just as easily as it attaches identity to a physical body. In either case, you are still ego-bound to the illusion of separateness.

In reality, there is no separation from God, who is, to repeat the words of Da Free John, the Condition of all conditions. I refer to Da Free John again at this point, because I find his teaching about the nature of enlightenment to be one of the most precise and comprehensive among contemporary spiritual teachers. The radical state of consciousness to which he and all sages draw devotees is that condition prior to any manifestation of substance or experience whatsoever, including the most spatially and temporally extended superphysical body operating in the most ethereal realm of existence. God realization, Da Free John teaches, is dissolving into that which lights creation in all states, conditions, and forms. It is literally becoming nobody. In the state of full enlightenment, no separate self is left, not even a soul. Even the idea that we are bodies and souls is illusory: all is God and only God. When we realize this, Da Free John declares in *The Enlightenment of the Whole Body*,° we are dissolved in it. "Ultimately, we vanish—not only out of present sight, as in death, but out of the entire space-time cycle of action and reaction, or illusion and change."

For the enlightened ones, the self is no longer limited or bound. The spark of God within each of us has, in them, been fanned into the divine fire that consumes the person/personality totally on every level of being, and in the process all sense of separateness is seen to be an illusion. Upon death, the person and the personality are simply no more.

When there is no more separation, where can you go? Nowhere—which is the same as saying that you are already everywhere, even though "you" as a separate personality—whether embodied or disembodied—no longer exist. You have returned to the One which is the all, the Ground of Being from which creation in all its forms on all levels of existence springs. You are God, just as you have been all along. But now you are conscious of it. Now you recognize yourself. And you recognize yourself in all else—in people, in trees, mountains and stars, in ghosts, angels and demons, in everything that is. The infinite variety of forms and conditions of existence, including all that we conventionally call life and death, are merely aspects of yourself. Living and dying are simply different aspects of being—the one perfect, formless, unbound being from which all existence arises in all its forms.

Thus liberated from illusion, you recognize that God is the dynamic of history. God is the motive power that "makes the world go round" and moves every individual, however much he may resist, into a love affair with the divine. It may take many lives for the illusion of separateness

---

°Available from Dawn Horse Book Depot, P.O. Box 3680, Clearlake Highlands, CA 95422.

to be dispelled (although it is possible to do so now, in this life), but God is in no hurry. God has all the time in the universe. And it's only God on stage anyway. There is no other. In reality, there is no one to die. And no one to be born. Therefore, how can you die since you were never born? "Before Abraham was, I am."

A statement by Da Free John is appropriate to quote here because it shows clearly the nature of death from the universal point of view which he, a God-realized teacher, presents:

> There are great dimensions, great cosmic possibilities. You may drift into them and enjoy a kind of mortality that seems immortal. There are worlds in which longevity is intensified almost to the point of immortality. But it is not literal immortality. Those very worlds themselves are declining and going through cycles, so there is no fixed condition. . . . There are siddha-worlds and angelic worlds, endless kinds of worlds which cannot be conceived from the point of view of man. If you look out into the night at those infinite numbers of stars and planets, what you see is just one little tiny galaxy. Through a large telescope you can see thousands of galaxies, in which there are billions of possible worlds. And yet these are only those visible within this little portion of the light spectrum, this narrow little vibration in which we conceive visibility. . . .
> The event of a human death in the midst of all of that is nothing. . . . It just seems important from the point of view of fear.

In *The Enlightenment of the Whole Body*, he states:

> The primary initiation that leads to human maturity is the confrontation with mortal fear. Only when the ultimate frustration that is death has been fully considered and felt and understood as a process can the individual live without self-protective and self-destructive fears. Only in intuitive freedom from the threat and fear of death is the individual capable of constant love of Life and also transcendence of the frustrating and self-binding effects of daily experience. Only in freedom from mortal recoil is the individual capable of ecstasy under all conditions.

Elsewhere Da Free John remarks, "Fear of death is fear of surrender to Infinity." Fear is a by-product of the human sense of separation, of limitation and boundary upon our consciousness. The ego is essentially *bound consciousness.* Those boundaries are self-created and then clung to fiercely. But when there is no boundary, there is only un-bound awareness, cosmic consciousness—enlightenment. And in the enlightened condition of realizing your essential self as one and the same with God, all fear vanishes. Bliss and wisdom alone remain as gifts from your best friend, death, which is really only a form of God that you failed to realize and which God used to "bring you home." As the ancient wisdom of the Upanishads puts it, "Wherever there is other, there is fear." Enlightenment is knowing God as "the love that casts out all fear."

For those who wish to examine this more, the experience of enlightenment in various sacred traditions has been very usefully explored in a short, easily-read book entitled *Coming Home* by Lex Hixon (Jeremy Tarcher, 1988). My own book, *The Highest State of Consciousness* (Anchor Books, 1972) also examines the experience through the writings of various ancient and modern authors in both the scientific and spiritual fields, as does my recent anthology, *What Is Enlightenment?* (Jeremy P. Tarcher, 1985).

The clearest and most brilliant elaborations of the nature of enlightenment can be found in the writings of Ken Wilber, author of *The Spectrum of Consciousness* (Quest Books, 1977) and former editor of *ReVision Journal.* I do not think it an overstatement to describe him as the Einstein of consciousness research. His theoretical formu-lation is fully equal in importance and insightfulness to Einstein's famous equation, and they both achieved their conceptual breakthrough at the same young age. Wilber' work establishes a new school of psychology, Spectr psychology, which elegantly synthesizes *all* other chological schools and traditions—and philosophy as Moreover, Spectrum psychology does this in a w? damages none while uniting all in a concepti

integrates East and West, as well as the various psycho-
therapies within Western psychology.

The basic ideas of Spectrum psychology have recently
been presented by Wilber in a simplified popular version
called *No Boundary* (Shambhala Publications, 1983). Two
works of his, *The Atman Project* (Quest Books, 1980) and
Up from Eden (Anchor Books, 1981) establish Spectrum
psychology as the high water mark of modern investiga-
tions into the nature of mind and consciousness. Such an
important breakthrough in noetic research deserves the full
attention of all fields of knowledge. I predict that later
generations will acknowledge Wilber as one of the greatest
minds of history.

What does Spectrum psychology say that is so important
for us here? A series of short quotations from *The Atman
Project* will serve to answer. *Atman*, by the way, is a Sanskrit
term meaning "self" or "the deepest center of the individual" beyond ego and personal characteristics. In the
tradition from which the term arose, Atman is said to be
identical with Brahman. In other words, the essence of
everyone is God or, as Wilber puts it, Atman is "ultimate
Unity consciousness in only God."

Before there were Many, there was—is—and always will
be—One. We come from God and return to God. In
between, however, is the story of mankind's fall and redemption—the mighty evolutionary drama in which unity
differentiates into multiplicity and sets about re-membering
itself. *The Atman Project* is "the attempt to *recover* the
basic unity of ultimate, pre-birth and pre-historical Atman-
consciousness, but an attempt at re-union carried out in
ways that necessarily prevent it and force successively
higher substitute gratifications and symbolic unions."

Those substitute gratifications and symbolic unions are
what we call history—the ego's attempt to play God.

Each level of the spectrum [of consciousness] is constructed as a *symbolic substitute* for lost Unity, so that
ultimately each level of the spectrum is (prior to enlightenment) a substitute for Atman-consciousness. Nevertheless,
every individual, at every level of consciousness continues

to intuit that he is of one nature with the Godhead, but he distorts that intuition by applying it to his separate self. Not that his deepest Self is *already* God, timeless and eternal, but that his individual self *should* be God, immortal, cosmocentric, death-defying, and all-powerful—*that* is the Atman project. It is the *impossible* desire for one's individual self to be immortal and cosmocentric, but based on the otherwise *correct* intuition that one's prior nature is always already infinite and eternal, the Immortal One in all forms.

That is why we say the Atman project is both true and false: true, in that each individual *is* natively God, and constantly intuits that this is so; false, in that this intuition is perpetually displaced to the individual's separate self at all levels. Not the ego dissolved in God, but the ego trying to be God—that is the Atman project.

The Atman project, then, is a seeking of prior Unity in ways that prevent it—namely, as a separate self in space and time. Thus arises history and all the works of man in which he seeks to enthrone himself for eternity as an individual, telling himself that fame, status, power, wealth and so forth truly satisfy his longing for conscious reunion with the source of his being. But, says Wilber, "since the individual will not accept the death and sacrifice of his separate self sense, he cannot find true transcendence and unity consciousness."

It is the separate self sense—the ego—that flees death and seeks immortality. Why? Because death appears to be the end of individuality, and individuality is the only condition of existence which the ego can conceive or acknowledge as true. "The separate self sense, by definition, is a contraction against the open and infinite ground of unity consciousness (or, if you prefer, God-consciousness)." Death threatens to dissolve the separate self sense, and people therefore repress, deny, or openly fear death.

But the flight from death, Spectrum psychology asserts, is also a flight from Unity consciousness. This is another way of saying that our fear of death is a fear of recog- nizing and remembering ourselves as Atman, Only when an individual accepts the death and of his separate self sense will he find true transcendence and unity consciousness.

The Atman project, then, is the story of the life of every human being—of you and me and the human race itself. It is the essentially correct intuition of a prior and un-limited essence corrupted by its application to the separate self sense. Spectrum psychology does not merely expose the workings of the Atman project, however. It also shows how the Atman project can be undone, terminated, so that God, not ego, becomes recognized as the true center and ground of ourselves, permeating all levels of our existence —body, mind, and spirit. I cannot speak too highly of the importance of Wilber's accomplishment in developing Spectrum psychology, because it interfaces beautifully with modern psychologies, illuminating them but also surpassing and fulfilling them in the depths of the peren-nial wisdom.

At the beginning of this chapter I asked: Who or what dies? The answer should now be clear. Death is most fearsome because it threatens us with the loss of in-dividuality. But that individuality, that separateness of self is itself an illusion, and when an illusion dies, nothing is really and truly lost except the illusion. And what is an illusion? Only a misperception, a mistake in thinking, an error of mind. But what a sound and fury we humans make on the basis of an illusion. All the suffering, brutality, and grief of history can be traced to a little three-letter word: e-g-o.

Our fear of death is ultimately fear of enlightenment, of losing our sense of separate self, of merging with the All. On the deepest level of our existence, we are *already* merged, of course. But the illusion of separateness leads us to think otherwise.

To lose an illusion means only to see more clearly. That is the challenge of human existence: to see, to know, to be— as fully and truly as the god-in-hiding that we are. To drop the primal *e* and add the final *d*: from ego to god—that is what this book is ultimately about. Egoing, egoing, egone. And all that is left is All. What, then, is there to fear?

Appendix 1
Is Death Necessary?
The Prospects for
Physical Immortality

One way to eliminate the fear of death is to eliminate death itself. That is what immortalists propose.

Theoretically speaking, physical immortality is unprovable. Only at the end of time would you know for sure that you were immortal. You might be breezing along for the first thousand years or so—or even the first million or billion—and then, for whatever reason, you die. That's merely longevity, not immortality.

But there's no need to debate the fine points here. Probably you'd gladly settle for a lifetime of 300 or 3,000 years, agreeing with immortalist George Bernard Shaw that the extra years give us opportunity to grow in wisdom and to improve the *quality* of our years along with the quantity. If we ever invent the immortality pill, but there's nothing better to do than gossip idly at the local senior citizens center, it'll be a sad day for humanity.

Immortality, then, is an ideal, and since the emphasis in this book is on the *practical*, you may be wondering why I've included immortality. I have two reasons. First, the immortalist movement is practical because it presents a strong challenge to deeply entrenched attitudes toward death—attitudes which you yourself may share and which have contributed strongly toward the fear and anxiety you feel about death. Consider, for example, this comment

from A. Stuart Otto, chairman of The Committee for
Elimination of Death. Otto, a minister by occupation,
wrote recently in the Committee's bulletin:

> Human attitudes on most subjects are formed early, and,
> as life progresses they are increasingly conditioned into
> the psyche. The attitude toward death is no exception.
> Recently a group of children, ages seven through nine,
> were asked, "If you could live to be as old as you wanted,
> what age would you choose?" A dozen answers, ranging
> from 30 to 115, were listened to soberly.
>
> Then one girl replied, "A thousand." Everyone laughed.
> Why? Because already, at these tender ages, the children
> "know" that attainment of such an age is "impossible."

My second reason is: Immortalism presents a worthy
cause with which you can identify, not as a means of ego
glorification, and not as a way to cover up fear of dying,
but as a genuinely high-minded effort to relieve human
suffering, including your own. As Otto puts it, expressing
his personal opinion, the only real justification for extending life beyond the normal span is to provide more
time for the individual to make the transition from human-
hood to divinity. By rising above narrow egotism and the
state of consciousness which identifies with a mortal body,
you are free to work for human betterment, without
anxiety and without seeking reward or recognition. You
are a part of a movement that disregards racial, sexual,
national, religious, and economic labels. Immortalism,
therefore, offers a vehicle for some degree of self-
transcendence. It is a genuinely transpersonal endeavor,
although it should not be mistaken for a vehicle for enlightenment. Even if death were eliminated—and therefore
the fear of death—you would still hunger for union, for
ecstasy, for total transcendence of the separate self that
identifies with a physical body.

What specifically do immortalists say? Here are some
selected quotes.

"Physical immortality is the only cause you can't die for."

"Death is not inevitable. You don't have to die. The
two certainties—death and taxes—will be reduced to

one. Taxes no doubt will remain, but death will be conquered."

"Immortality will enrich your aliveness to no end."

"Conquest of death is the 'evolutionary summit' of human life."

"Death is status quo thinking. You program yourself for death."

"Live as though you were immortal. Your death urge is only a philosophy until you're dead."

"Death is an imposition on the human race, and no longer acceptable."

"The belief that death is inevitable is unhealthy to humans."

"There are people alive now who are never going to die."

"If it is natural to die, then to hell with nature. We must rise above nature. We must refuse to die."

"Some people want to achieve immortality through their works or their descendents. I prefer to achieve immortality by not dying."

The author of the last statement is comedian Woody Allen. Between him and Otto stand a host of philosophers, futurists, medical researchers, and writers who are serious proponents of immortalism. Efforts are going on apace to prolong life, reverse aging, replace worn-out organs, regenerate limbs, cryogenically freeze bodies until cures for fatal diseases are found, etc. Efforts are also being made to root out from society all unconscious "death thinking" such as, "I'm dead tired," "I thought I'd die laughing," "I'll remember it to my dying day," "If I live to be a hundred," "I'm tickled to death to see you," "He really slays me," "I was scared to death," etc.

What's the schedule for immortality? Immortalists are not in full agreement, but some medical researchers speak in terms of extending life spans by at least a decade or two by the end of this century, and to several hundred years and beyond by the end of the next. Other immortalists maintain that psychological and spiritual techniques offer the means to attain it right now.

If you'd like to know more about the immortalist

movement, read Alan Harrington's *The Immortalist* and other books you'll find in the library. Also, write for information to: The Committee for Elimination of Death, P.O. Box 696, San Marcos, CA 92069. And for practical instruction in yoga-based techniques claimed to offer immortality, write to: Life Unlimited, 301 Lyon Street, San Francisco, CA 94117:

Appendix 2

Self-Destruction versus Self-Sacrifice: Suicide and the Question of Identity

Every day, world wide, more than one thousand people take their own lives.

If death is so fearful, why do some people commit suicide? Why do they prefer to die than to live? There are many reasons for it—as many as there are different views of death. While some may fear it, they may fear life even more. The politician caught in law-breaking cannot stand public humiliation and so commits suicide, along with the financier whose fortune from investments is wiped out by the vicissitudes of the stock market. The jilted lover joins them, along with the "little kid on the block," who is mercilessly taunted by insensitive people.

Clearly, for some, death is preferable to living. It offers apparent release from suffering, shame, confusion, despair, meaninglessness. For others, however, death offers an avenue to honor, virtue, and triumph. To such people, death may also be preferable to living, although their reasons for self-inflicted loss of life are radically different from those of the tormented suicides.

Consider the example of Sona Kanwar, a 62-year-old Indian woman, who committed *suttee* in 1980 after her husband died. The ancient Hindu tradition, outlawed since the nineteenth century, calls for the wife to dress in her best clothes, wash her hands in water drawn from the sacred Ganges River, and then mount the funeral pyre on which her husband is to be cremated. When the pyre is lighted, husband and wife are united in death. In this case, Kanwar climbed atop the pyre, cradled her husband's head on her lap, and set the wood ablaze herself. Nothing was left but ashes.

The factor that connects these examples of glorious and inglorious suicide is the question of identity, central to overcoming fear of death *and* life: Who or what lives and dies?

In seeking to understand themselves and to give meaning to their existence, people develop a sense of identity—separate identity. As infants, they have no sense of differentiation. They are one with the all. But shortly after birth, early in infancy, they become aware of themselves as a body, a physical organism limited in time and space. This is the first sense of separate identity that develops, and it is the one that most people operate with well into adulthood. For those whose sense of self is principally as a body, a physical organism, death is perceived as the ultimate threat to their existence, and it becomes fearful.

Often, however, people grow to identify with something that transcends the gross flesh—something mental or something beyond the individual body. It may be a business success, social status, academic achievement, a special talent, a "good name." Take these accomplishments away and you've taken away their sense of identity. The individual becomes despondent and life becomes oppressive. Often suicide seems the only answer.

People may also identify with a cause that offers them identity and gives meaning to their existence. In such cases, fear of dying is greatly allayed, even to the point of self-destruction. To kill yourself for love or for a social struggle appears glorious, inspiring, even desirable—a form of immortality. History and literature are filled with examples of people who willingly embraced death as a means of self-transcendence. Romeo and Juliet, for example, epitomize the idea of dying for romantic love. Their sense of self was so intimately bound up in one another that suicide seemed preferable to living without each other. This is the case with every couple whose death—whether at a Lover's Leap or by any other means—is their way of responding to apparently insurmountable barriers to their love.

Often people are inspired to suicide not by romance but by a sense of social or political need. Martyrs such as Nathan Hale undertook "suicide missions" and gave their lives for something they believed was important to society. At Masada, Jewish zealots resisted Roman rule after the fall of Jerusalem and willingly died for their allegiance to political Judaism. Many Christian saints are famed for martyrdom in the name of their faith. Likewise, Buddhist monks in the Vietnamese war immolated themselves as a symbol of resistance to religious oppression. And remember the Alamo. Unlike cases of despondent suicide, these people are revered as heroes and wise men.

Usually, that is. They may also be considered fools or dupes. Take the case of Japanese kamikaze pilots. Their identity was intimately bound up in the Emperor, who was himself not so much a person as a personage—the living symbol of Japan as an empire ruling the world through divine destiny. Thus, kamikaze pilots had little fear of dying because, first, they grew up in a culture that routinely accepted the notion of postmortem survival, ancestor worship and *bushido*, the way of the warrior-samurai; and, second, through identification with the Emperor/empire, their sense of self doubly transcended regret over personal extinction. An excerpt from the diary of a kamikaze pilot, as quoted in *The Divine Wind*, illustrates this point:

> I am actually a member at last of the Kamikaze Special Attack Corps. My life will be rounded out in the next thirty days. My chance will come! Death and I are waiting. The training and practice have been rigorous, but it is worth while if we can die beautifully and for a cause.

These volunteers who flew their lethal payload into the enemy target were enthusiastic, almost ecstatic, in their willingness to sacrifice their lives. As one wrote home:

Cadet X was dropped from the list of those assigned to take part in the sortie, upon my arrival. Cannot help feeling sorry for him.

Please congratulate me. I have been given a splendid opportunity to die. This is my last day. The destiny of our homeland hinges on the decisive battle in the seas to the south where I shall fall like a blossom from a radiant cherry tree.

Such ecstatic faith, John Hinton tells us in *Dying*, can evidently overcome all doubts and fears about death. If this is coupled with a belief in predestination, the prospect of dying is further eased because joy and grief are already ordained. Neither struggle nor distress can alter the immutable.

More recently, the world witnessed what by all accounts is a tragic story: the Jonestown massacre. Jim Jones, a charismatic but psychopathic megalomaniac, exhorted—even coerced—his naive followers to suicide through a variety of mind-manipulating techniques based on faith and fear. For hundreds of the Jonestown, Guyana, residents whose identities were fatally entwined with Jones and who had been conditioned into believing that violent death awaited them in the near future anyway, it became better to "die with dignity," as Jones put it, than to be shot down like animals by "the enemy." That enemy never existed except in Jones' twisted mind, but he convinced his followers such as Bea Grubbs to state in writing that "I would never betray you, no matter what. . . . I shall not beg for mercy either in that last moment. I shall proudly die for a proud reason."

Thus, death by one's own hand is not an easy matter to judge. One person's faith is another's foolishness.

How can we distinguish one from the other? For example, is there wisdom in Jesus' teaching: "Greater love hath no man than this, that a man lay down his life for his friends" (John 15:13)? Was Jesus' death on the cross the act of a paranoid schizophrenic, as Albert Schweitzer maintained in *The Quest for the Historical Jesus*, or was it a supreme act of selfless, transpersonal love?

From the perspective of this book, it was the latter, of course. The crucifixion to which Jesus willingly submitted was self-sacrifice, not self-destruction. The crucial difference is that Jesus had a clear sense of identification with God. "Crucial" means not only of supreme importance, it also means the final determination of a doubtful issue.

If there is any doubtful issue for people, it is the issue of identity. Everyone wonders to some degree, "Who am I?" The more serious ones pursue the question consciously through all the forms of human enquiry and endeavor, developing a sense of identity that is more and more self-transcendent because it is based on a wider and clearer perception of reality. Nevertheless, as *The Atman Project* shows, that identity is still limited, incomplete, a substitute for God if it is not the Supreme Identity realized by a Christ, a Buddha, a Da Free John. Whether it is self-identity conceived in immature forms such as teenagers show for film stars and popular singers, or in more mature—but still adolescent—forms such as adults often show for political leaders, religious figures, cultural movements, and spiritual teachers, that sense of self is still based on the person trying to play God rather than realizing his prior identity with God.

Jesus' death was *crucial*—pun intended—because it was on the cross (Latin, *cruc*) that he made the final determination of the doubtful issue of separation from God ("My God, my God, why hast thou forsaken me?") that was of supreme importance for self-deluded, suffering humanity. His realization of godhood was not the delusion of exclusive divinity, which was Jim Jones' downfall. Rather, it was the realization of *non*exclusive divinity—the recognition that *already* we are being lived by God, however much we are unaware of it, and that someday in the fullness of time *all* will be consciously "one in Christ" or the Christ consciousness. *That*, rather than some worldly political rule, would be the redemption of fallen humanity, and for that Jesus sacrificed himself.

The aim of a confused, unhappy person who commits suicide is self-destruction. But someone who is certain of the nature of his existence, and who therefore is happy in God, cannot be said to aim at self-destruction, even though he commits suicide. His act is self-sacrifice. His aim is to teach, to inspire, to protect, to nurture the lives of his fellow humans who, unlike him, are ignorant and suffering. For this he willingly casts off the body, should it be necessary. The forms that self-sacrifice take are many, but the purpose is always the same: to awaken people to their true identity.

Suicide, then, has two forms. Self-destruction is the act of someone suffering from a desperate case of mistaken identity. It is different from self-sacrifice. Self-destruction is based on fear, self-sacrifice is based on love.

Short of that realization, a person will find himself no better off after committing suicide than before. As I said earlier, death does not automatically make a saint of a sinner or a sage of a fool. The evidence for life after death shows that confusion and unhappiness do not magically disappear in the postmortem state. The suicide attempters interviewed by Ring and Moody in their studies of near-death cases told of realizing that death is no answer, that self-destruction is an illusion, and that life is to be lived, not avoided or escaped, no matter how oppressive or doubtful it may seem. Reincarnation research also supports this position. The whole purpose of returning to the earth plane, life after life, is to become aware of our true nature— infinite, eternal, indestructible, one with God, the self of All.

Appendix 3
A Resource List for Death Education

I have deliberately omitted most books about the nature of postmortem existence and the evidence for immortality. The purpose of this list is to provide *practical* guidance for those who want information about how to die and how to assist the dying. Although some of the books are philosophical or theoretical about the afterlife, they nevertheless contain material I feel is useful and pragmatic.

Books

Pandit Usharbudh Arya, *Meditation and the Art of Dying.* Himalayan International Institute of Yoga, Science and Philosophy: Honesdale, PA, 1979. *Offers instruction in meditation designed to overcome fear of dying.*

Richard W. Boerstler, *Letting Go: A Holistic and Meditative Approach to Living and Dying.* Associates in Thanatology: 115 Blue Rock Road, South Yarmouth, MA 02664. *Describes an ancient Tibetan Buddhist practice called comeditation, by which the dying can be assisted to reduce pain and stress, moving toward "clear mind and peaceful heart."* (See Videotape section.)

Lisa Carlson, *Caring for Your Own Dead.* Upper Access Publishers: P.O. Box 457, Hinesburg, VT 05461.

Guidelines on how loved ones can play a greater role in planning a funeral and carrying it out, with state-by-state legal requirements described.

Earlyne Chaney, *The Mystery of Death and Dying*. Samuel Weiser: York Beach, ME, 1988. Subtitled "Initiation at the Moment of Death;" it offers practical information on how to die.

Melita Denning and Osborne Phillips, *Astral Projection*. Llewellyn Publications: St. Paul, MN, 1987. *Offers practical instructions for fully conscious out-of-body travel and return, plus guidance about the astral world.*

Debra Duda, *Coming Home: A Guide to Dying at Home with Dignity*. Aurora Press: New York, 1987. *Tells how to make a dying person's final weeks as comfortable and meaningful as possible.*

W.Y. Evans-Wenz, *The Tibetan Book of the Dead*. Oxford Press: London, 1960. *A classic guide to postmortem states from the perspective of attaining enlightenment through death and being liberated from the cycle of reincarnation by realizing the nature of self. Contains useful commentaries by Carl Jung and Lama Govinda.*

Anya Foos-Graber, *Deathing: An Intelligent Alternative for the Final Moments of Life*. Nicolas-Hays: York Beach, ME, 1987. *The section entitled "A Manual of Deathing" offers a variety of techniques for preparing oneself for the actual moment of death.*

Francesca Fremantle and Chogyam Trungpa, *The Tibetan Book of the Dead*. Shambhala: Boulder, CO, 1975. *Another excellent translation of this classic work on death education.*

E.J. Gold, *The Lazy Man's Guide to Death & Dying*. IDHHB Publishing: P.O. Box 370, Nevada City, CA 95959, 1983. *A humorously serious work offering exact instructions on how to confront the symptoms of death, plus detailed material on how to choose rebirth.*

————, *New American Book of the Dead*. IDHHB Publishing: P.O. Box 370, Nevada City, CA 95959, 1981. *Detailed description of the Intermediate State between death and rebirth.*

Derek Humphrey, *Let Me Die Before I Wake.* Hemlock Society: P.O. Box 66218, Los Angeles, CA 90066. *A guide to "self-deliverance" (voluntary euthanasia or suicide) for the terminally ill. Tells how to obtain potentially lethal drugs and the amounts needed.*

Da Free John, *Easy Death: Talks and Essays on the Inherent and Ultimate Transcendence of Death and Everything Else.* Dawn Horse Press: Clearlake, CA, 1983. *An extraordinarily powerful book with radical insight into the nature of death and postmortem states. See Part V, "How to Serve the Dying."*

M.V. Kamath, *Philosophy of Death & Dying.* Himalayan International Institute of Yoga, Science and Philosophy: Honesdale, PA, 1978. *Inspiring, heroic stories of great men and women from diverse cultures and the way they died.*

Philip Kapleau, *The Wheel of Death.* Harper & Row: New York, 1971. *Practical instructions about dying within the perspective of the Zen tradition.*

Stanley Keleman, *Living Your Dying.* Random House: New York, 1974. *His "Five-Breath Meditation" is a short, simple but powerful exercise for beginning to release fear of dying.*

Stephen Levine, *A Gradual Awakening.* Anchor Press: New York, 1979. *A teacher of meditation, who works extensively with the dying, offers insightful and practical commentary.*

————, *Who Dies?* Anchor Press: New York, 1982. *A sensitive, poetic "investigation of conscious living and conscious dying."*

Lama Lodö, *Bardo Teachings.* Snow Lion: Ithaca, NY, 1987. *A tantric Buddhist manual on how to traverse the stages of death without fear.*

Florence Wagner McClain, *A Practical Guide to Past Life Regression.* Llewellyn: St. Paul, MN, 1986. *A transpersonal approach to past-life recall that is both spiritual and practical, helping people to understand death.*

Marjorie Casebier McCoy, *To Die with Style.* Abingdon Press: Nashville, TN, 1974. *A philosophic approach* to self-examination, with practical exercises, that looks at death "not primarily as a thing to be suffered but rather as an action to be anticipated and prepared for."

George W. Meek, *After We Die, What Then?* Metascience Foundation, P.O. Box 747, Franklin, NC 28734. *Appendix E, "How to Die," contains useful information.*

Paul S. Minear, *Death Set to Music: Masterworks by Bach, Brahms, Penderewski, Bernstein.* John Knox: Atlanta, 1986. *An approach to understanding death through the works of four musical classics.*

Ernest Morgan, *A Manual of Death Education and Simple Burial.* Celo Press: Brunswick, NC 28714, 1980. (Retitled *Dealing Creatively with Death* in later expanded editions.) *Perhaps the best overview of death and dying from the standpoint of preparing for it legally, financially, and humanely.*

Glenn H. Mullin, *Death and Dying: The Tibetan Tradition.* Routledge & Kegan Paul/Arkana: Boston, MA, 1986. *The chapter on "The Yoga of Consciousness Transference" is especially important.*

Carol Parrish-Harra, *A New Age Handbook of Death & Dying.* DeVorss: Marina del Rey, CA, 1982. *A very nice overview of death and dying with guidance for helping the dying and the bereaved.*

Bo Yin Ra, *The Book on Life Beyond.* The Kober Press: San Francisco, 1978. *The chapter on "The Art of Dying" contains succinct, sage advice on how to prepare for death and navigate the afterlife realms.*

Swami Rama, *Life Here and Hereafter.* Himalayan International Institute of Yoga, Science and Philosophy: Glenview, IL, 1976. *An inspired series of lectures, based on the Hindu classic Kathopanishad, which distill its spiritual essence into modern form, emphasizing the nature of consciousness and self-realization.*

Lati Rinbochay, *Death, Intermediate State and Rebirth.* Snow Lion: Ithaca, New York, 1980. *Discusses the stages of death and dying from a Tibetan Buddhist viewpoint.*

D. Scott Rogo, *Leaving the Body.* Prentice-Hall: Englewood

Cliffs, NJ, 1983. *Eight different systems to enable one to astral project are covered.*

Harry van Bommel, *Choices: For People Who Have a Terminal Illness*. NC Press Limited: 260 Richmond St. West, Toronto, Ontario, Canada M5V 1W5. *Discusses patient autonomy in a rational, organized manner that is practical and user-friendly.*

John White, *A Practical Guide to Death and Dying*. Theosophical Publishing House: Wheaton, IL, 1980 (rev. 1988). *A step-by-step program for freeing yourself of fear and anxiety about your own demise.*

Articles

Sherry Baker, "Death Rehearsal," *Omni*, June 1987 (on p. 96 in "Antimatter" section).

Richard Boerstler, "Meditation and the Dying Process," *Journal of Humanistic Psychology*, Vol. 26, No. 2, Spring 1986. *Essentially a summary of the author's book* Letting Go.

Brother David Steindl-Rast, "Learning to Die," *Parabola*, Vol. 1, No. 1.

Frank C. Tribbe and Lila DiZefalo, "Helping Someone Die." *Spiritual Frontiers*, Vol. 19, No. 2, Spring 1987.

Audiotapes and Videotapes

Richard W. Boerstler, *Letting Go: A Holistic and Meditative Approach to Death and Dying*. Associates in Thanatology: 115 Blue Rock Road, South Yarmouth, MA 02664. Videotape (30 minutes, 1/2-inch color VHS). *A demonstration of the ancient Tibetan Buddhist practice of comeditation.* (See Books section.)

Hugh B. Montgomery, *Summing Up and Farewell*. Pat Montgomery, 187 Ridge Road, Bailey, CO 80421. Videotape (60 minutes, 1/2-inch black-and-white VHS). *A summation by Hugh Montgomery, shortly before he*

*died, of the meaning of life and its relation to death,
including comments on how to assist the dying.*
Carol Parrish-Harra, *Meditation Plus*. Village Bookstore,
Sparrowhawk Village, P.O. Box 1274, Tahlequah, OK
74465. Audiotape. *Guided meditations for relaxation
and reducing anxiety in the dying.*

Courses

Don't overlook conventional sources such as training at
schools of religion, medical schools, nursing schools,
hospice training courses, and other centers of learning.
All of these address the issues of death and dying in their
training of students as caregivers and counselors.

Transit Practitioner's Course—*teaches you to be competent
in dealing with those who are dying, to prepare them
for the Intermediate State and to maintain a strong,
close contact with them throughout the complete Transit
cycle.* IDHHB Publishing: P.O. Box 370, Nevada City,
CA 95959.

Other

Donalyn Gross, *Grief Songs: Greeting Cards for the
Terminally Ill.* Available from Donalyn Gross at 471
Allen Park Road, Springfield, MA 01118. *Designed by a
social worker-thanatologist to acknowledge the fact of
someone's death with honesty, sensitivity, and even
humor. This wide variety of cards is for the dying to
send and to receive. For a free pamphlet, send a self-
addressed stamped envelope.*
Hemlock Society, P.O. Box 66218, Los Angeles, CA 90066.
*Supports the option of active voluntary euthanasia for
the terminally ill and promotes a climate of public
opinion which is tolerant of the right of people who are
terminally ill to end their own lives in a planned manner.
Publishes a quarterly international newsletter.*

Appendix 4
The Right to Die—
A Modest Proposal

One of my friends is Helen G. Ansley, who is nearly 90. She spoke at a Phenix Society meeting (see Chapter 12) recently on the issue of the right to die. "What's Wrong with Dying?" she asked as the title of her talk. Advocating euthanasia as a means of preserving a person's dignity and financial estate, she stated that it was both ethical and humane to allow a person to choose the time and manner of death.

Because I found her "modest proposal" so thoughtful, I offer this slightly modified newspaper account of it for your consideration in overcoming fear of death.

"Everybody does it, but nobody talks about it"—meaning planning ahead for your own death—says 88-year-old Helen G. Ansley of Fairhaven, Massachusetts. "Why don't we explore better ways of dying? Why don't we create suitable environments for a good death—a death with dignity?"

Ansley spoke about "What's Wrong with Dying?" at [location].

"We plan ahead for the other major events in our life—education, job, marriage, children, vacations, retirement," Mrs. Ansley said. "Moreover, lots of people earn a living

191

helping us plan for those events and celebrate them. But any attempt to plan for a good death for ourselves is considered a sign of deep depression, of mental illness, and we're liable to be turned over—by a well-meaning close relative—to the care of a psychiatrist, whose responsibility is to prevent any suicide attempt."

In some parts of the country it is a crime to help anyone, regardless of age or quality of life, to plan their own death, she noted, adding that society demands that health professionals prolong life, no matter what the cost.

As a result, there is no place to go to die at a time of one's own choosing, Ansley remarked. "There's no place to plan to spend the last week or ten days making your own funeral arrangements, saying goodbye to friends, giving away your remaining treasures when you're sure you no longer need them. No place for a final celebration, surrounded by a few people who would rejoice with you in the achievement of a good death at an appropriate time in a peaceful manner without the huge expense of an intensive care bed in a hospital or a long drawn-out decline in a nursing home. Can't we have a place where mentally alert people can plan to go when they're ready to die? Some smart business person ought to make a lot of money out of a 'last resort' like that. It could also be described as a 'finishing school.' I'd call it The Way Out Inn."

Ansley, who has lectured all over the nation, injected a wry sense of humor into her talk. Several years ago, she said, she wrote this:

Why Not Die Laughing?

The high cost of living is merely a joke.
It's the high cost of dying that's keeping us broke!
The doctors and lawyers must all have their share
And those horrible prices for nursing home care!
The law won't permit any person to kill us
But any and all are encouraged to bill us!

Ansley has been a pioneer of one sort or another throughout her adult life. A 1921 graduate of Smith College, she married, raised a family, and became a widow in 1974. In between she was involved in adult education, community mental health care, world federation, the peace movement, holistic health, creative aging, and, most recently, planned dying.

She contends that one should realistically face the inevitable, not morbidly, but creatively. "Why not view death as a celebration?" she suggested. "Does it really have to be slow and painful and sad? I doubt it."

Ansley expressed her thoughts on what she calls "creative dying" in a recent poem:

A Last Resort

I wish there were a place for gracious dying,
A high place with a distant view
Where we could gather for a celebration
Of life and death and friendships, old and new.
I'd like a place where there would be good music,
Good food and wine—and laughter, games and fun—
And quiet talk with friends, and good discussion
Of what will happen when this life is done.

Helen Ansley can be reached at the Bradford-Russell Home, 62 Center Street, Fairhaven, Massachusetts 02719, tel. 617-991-2375.

About the Author

John White, M.A.T., is an internationally-known author, editor, and educator in the fields of consciousness research, parascience, and higher human development. He has held positions as Director of Education for the Institute of Noetic Sciences, a research organization founded by Apollo 14 astronaut Edgar Mitchell to study human potential for personal and planetary transformation, and as President of Alpha Logics, a school for self-directed growth in body, mind, and spirit.

He is author of *Pole Shift, Everything You Want to Know about TM*, and a children's book, *The Christmas Mice*. He has also edited a number of anthologies, including *The Highest State of Consciousness, What Is Meditation?, Frontiers of Consciousness, Psychic Exploration, Other Worlds/Other Universes, Future Science, Relax, Kundalini, Evolution and Enlightenment, Psychic Warfare—Fact or Fiction?,* and *What Is Enlightenment?* His books have been translated into various languages. His writing has appeared in magazines and newspapers such as *The New York Times, Saturday Review, Esquire, Omni, Reader's Digest, Science Digest,* Chicago *Sun-Times*, Philadelphia *Inquirer*, and San Francisco *Chronicle*.

White holds a Bachelor of Arts degree from Dartmouth College and a Master of Arts in teaching from Yale University. He has taught English and journalism on the secondary and college levels, and is on the boards of various academic and research organizations. He is also on the editorial boards of various scholarly journals and popular magazines, including *New Realities, ReVision, Yoga Journal, Venture Inward, Body Mind Spirit, Journal of Near-Death Studies,* and *Mind-Expander*. He writes a monthly column for *Science of Mind*. He has lectured at various colleges and universities throughout the U.S. and Canada, and has made numerous radio and television appearances.

He and his wife Barbara have four children and live at 60 Pound Ridge Road, Cheshire, Connecticut 06410.

We publish books on:

Healing, Health and Diet ● Occultism and Mysticism ● Transpersonal Psychology Philosophy ● Religion ● Reincarnation Theosophical Philosophy ● Yoga and Meditation

Other books of possible interest include:

And a Time to Die *by Mark Pelgrin*
Search for meaning in life and approaching death.

The Healing Energy of Love *by John Allen*
Deals with overcoming grief and conquering fear of death.

Life after Death *by C.W. Leadbeater*
How theosophy unveils it.

Mastering the Problems of Living *by Haridas Chaudhuri*
How to overcome depression, anxiety, and despair.

A Matter of Personal Survival *by Michael Marsh*
Answers the question: What happens to me after I die?

Our Last Adventure *by E. Lester Smith*
Common-sense guide to death by an eminent scientist.

Through the Gateway of Death *by Geoffrey Hodson*
A study of process of death and nature of life after death.

Transition Called Death *by Charles Hampton*
Physical and psychological effects of dying and death.

Available from:
The Theosophical Publishing House
306 W. Geneva Road, Wheaton, Illinois 60187